THE
EVERYTHING®
LOGIC
PUZZLES BOOK
VOLUME 1

Dear Reader,

Welcome to my collection of 200 logic puzzles, all designed to get you involved in systematic thinking. You might occasionally become frustrated, but I believe you will never get discouraged, because I wrote this book to impart to you how truly enjoyable and rather straightforward logical thinking is.

For this reason, I have taken absolutely nothing for granted. Even if you are an inveterate puzzle solver, you might appreciate my illustrations and explanations. You will find that each chapter is organized systematically. Each one focuses on a specific type of puzzle, organized in increasing order of difficulty. Also, each individual puzzle is completely explained at the back. The Answers section thus provides much more than just answers—it explains the solution to each puzzle.

I have always been passionate about puzzles and what they imply for all of us, both individually and historically. Hopefully, this book will convey to you the same type of excitement I have always felt in this arena of human intelligence.

Marcel Danesi, PhD

Welcome to the EVERYTHING® Series!

These handy, accessible books give you all you need to tackle a difficult project, gain a new hobby, comprehend a fascinating topic, prepare for an exam, or even brush up on something you learned back in school but have since forgotten.

You can choose to read an Everything® book from cover to cover or just pick out the information you want from our four useful boxes: e-questions, e-facts, e-alerts, e-ssentials. We give you everything you need to know on the subject, but throw in a lot of fun stuff along the way, too.

We now have more than 400 Everything® books in print, spanning such wide-ranging categories as weddings, pregnancy, cooking, music instruction, foreign language, crafts, pets, New Age, and so much more. When you're done reading them all, you can finally say you know Everything®!

PUBLISHER Karen Cooper

MANAGING EDITOR Lisa Laing

COPY CHIEF Casey Ebert

ASSISTANT PRODUCTION EDITOR Jo-Anne Duhamel

ACQUISITIONS EDITOR Zander Hatch

SENIOR DEVELOPMENT EDITOR Brett Palana-Shanahan

EVERYTHING® SERIES COVER DESIGNER Erin Alexander

THE EVERYTHING® LOGIC PUZZLES BOOK

VOLUME 1

200 puzzles to increase
your brain power

Marcel Danesi, PhD

Adams Media
New York London Toronto Sydney New Delhi

I would like to dedicate this book to my three wonderful grandchildren, Alex, Sarah, and Charlotte, who
have solved the puzzle of existence for me!

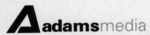

Adams Media
An Imprint of Simon & Schuster, Inc.
57 Littlefield Street
Avon, Massachusetts 02322

An Everything® Series Book.
Everything® and everything.com® are registered trademarks of Simon &
Schuster, Inc.

First Adams Media trade paperback edition JULY 2017

ADAMS MEDIA and colophon are trademarks of Simon and Schuster.

For information about special discounts for bulk purchases,
please contact Simon & Schuster Special Sales at 1-866-506-1949 or
business@simonandschuster.com.

The Simon & Schuster Speakers Bureau can bring authors to your live event. For
more information or to book an event contact the Simon & Schuster Speakers
Bureau at 1-866-248-3049 or visit our website at www.simonspeakers.com.

Interior design by Colleen Cunningham

Manufactured in the United States of America

10 9 8 7 6 5 4 3 2 1

ISBN 978-1-5072-0414-6

Contents

Introduction 9

Chapter 1: Card Logic Puzzles **11**
The Missing Card 12
The Odd Card Out 24
Card-Logic Mayhem 33

Chapter 2: Doublets **39**
Basic Doublets 40
Doublets Meet Anagrams 45
Doublet Mayhem 51

Chapter 3: Word Squares **53**
Three-by-Three Squares 54
Four-by-Four Squares 59
Five-by-Five Squares 63

Chapter 4: Word Logic Puzzles **67**
The Missing Word 68
The Odd Word Out 75
Word-Logic Mayhem 80

Chapter 5: Logical Deductions **83**
Deduction Puzzles 84
Truth Tellers and Liars 98
Drawing-Out Logic 104

Chapter 6: Domino Logic Puzzles **107**

The Missing Domino 108

The Odd Domino Out 117

Dominoes Meet Cards 125

Chapter 7: Number Logic Puzzles **131**

The Missing Number 132

Number-Letter Codes 137

Anything Goes 144

Chapter 8: Lie Detection Puzzles **147**

Who's the Culprit? 148

Who's the Culprit This Time? 153

Misleading Labels 160

Answers **164**

Chapter 1 164

Chapter 2 171

Chapter 3 174

Chapter 4 178

Chapter 5 184

Chapter 6 195

Chapter 7 207

Chapter 8 214

Acknowledgments

I thank my wonderful agent and longtime friend Grace Freedson for making this book possible. As they say today, "Grace, you're the best." I also want to express my gratitude to Zander Hatch, my editor at Simon & Schuster, for his advice and support. He has made it easy for me to do the very best I can do in puzzle creation. Thank you. Needless to say, any infelicities that this book may contain are my sole responsibility.

Introduction

Logical thinking does not come easy. Unlike instincts, which allow you to react to stimuli intuitively, you were not born with the ability to reason things out logically. Such thinking is an achievement that needs to be nurtured. Enter logic puzzles, which have been played since the dawn of history to foster this very form of thinking. Logic puzzles are simply conundrums that play with pattern, arrangement, and principles of organization. They reveal what it means to deduce, infer, or conclude something from a given set of facts, but in a fun way. Logic puzzles involve the same kind of thinking that has been the source of many great achievements, from science and mathematics to storytelling.

Most people are not aware that they are solving problems in logic from the moment they get up. For example, you wake up one morning and can't find your keys. Frustrated, you start looking randomly for them. But in reality you should stop and reason out the situation logically. First ask yourself:

Did I have the keys with me when I got home?

Answer: Yes, or I wouldn't have been able to open the door.

Where did I likely put them after that?

Answer: In my pocket.

Is that where they might be?

Answer: Yes, found them.

The same reasoning processes apply to the puzzles in this book. You will have to ask questions such as, *Where does this belong? What comes after this?* and so on. This book aims to get your logical mind working on all cylinders. Each chapter focuses on a specific genre of puzzle, and the puzzles are organized from easy to difficult within each section of a chapter. Also, because some kinds of puzzles may be new to you, each puzzle genre is illustrated at the beginning.

There is a large element of common sense involved in solving puzzles. But it is also true that without a basic understanding of how logical thinking unfolds, and what techniques can be employed to grow and sustain it, the ability to accurately solve puzzles will not emerge. Luckily, this book gives you an opportunity to gain practice in solving logic puzzles and build the techniques you'll need to solve other puzzles with ease. If you have never done these types of puzzles or if you're looking to hone your puzzle skills, you're in for hours of "fun" logic. Enjoy!

CHAPTER 1

Card Logic Puzzles

I am sorry I have not learnt to play at cards. It is very useful in life: it generates kindness, and consolidates society.
—SAMUEL JOHNSON (1709–1784)

Using cards to play games most likely originated in imperial China or in Hindustan around C.E. 800. No one knows for certain how cards made their way to Europe, but they first appeared in Italy in the 1200s and became very popular there. From Italy, the cards quickly spread to other parts of Europe. The origin of the four suits can be traced to France in the 1500s. A clover leaf marked the suit called *trèfle*, known as the club in English. The tip of a pike stood for the *pique* suit, called the spade in English. A heart figure, called *coeur* (the French word for heart) is, of course, the modern heart suit. The fourth suit, called *carreau*, means square, but it is now named diamond because of its diamond-shaped spot. Cards are used not only to play games but also to hone one's logic skills. The games in this chapter will use them for this very reason.

The Missing Card

The puzzles in this section are designed to test your ability to decipher a pattern in a card arrangement. Specifically, you will have to figure out what card or cards are missing from the arrangement. Let's go through one together just to get started.

▶ ILLUSTRATION ◀

Two rows consisting of four cards each are laid out on a table as shown. Each card in Row A corresponds to a card in Row B in some exact way. Knowing this, what card is missing from Row B?

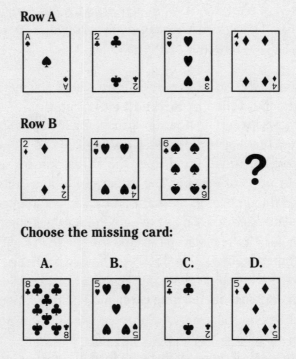

The answer is A. If you look carefully, you will see that the number value of each card in Row B is twice the one just above it in Row A. So below the four of diamonds in Row A, the missing card will have a number value of eight. Of the options given, only A works.

Got it? In the ten puzzles that follow look out for these things: (a) the type of layout that is involved, (b) the location of the card in it, (c) the suit of the card, and (d) the number value of the card. Of course, not all of these are always involved in the solution. You will have to be on your logical toes all the time. Have fun!

▸ EASY ◂

For the first three puzzles that follow you will be given hints, just to get you warmed up for the harder puzzles.

Puzzle 1

Two rows of cards are laid out on a table as shown. Which card is missing from the top row of the layout? **Hint:** focus on the order of the cards in each row.

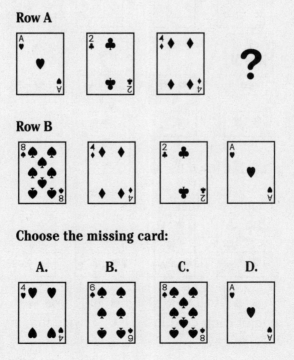

Row A

Row B

Choose the missing card:

A.   B.   C.   D.

Puzzle 2

Four hands have been dealt out to four different players from the standard fifty-two-card deck. The hands are shown in columns (from top to bottom). As it turns out, all four hands share an unexpected pattern. What card is missing from the third hand? **Hint:** each hand will have the same kinds of cards.

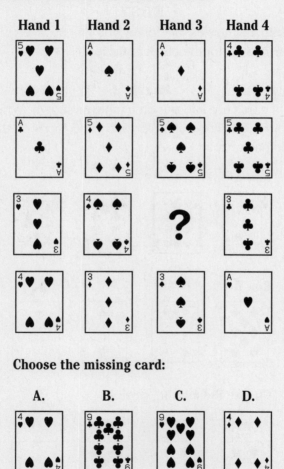

Choose the missing card:

A.   B.   C.   D.

Puzzle 3

The deck is shuffled again and another hand is dealt to the four players. The hands are shown in columns (from top to bottom). As it turns out, these four hands also share an unexpected pattern. What card is missing from the fourth hand? **Hint:** focus on the suits in each hand. Ignore the number values.

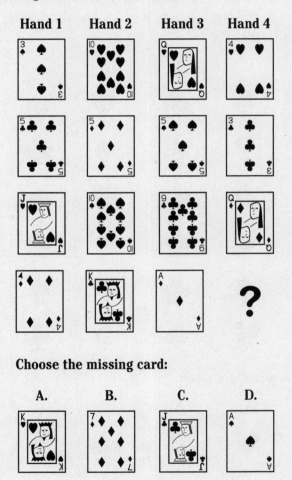

Choose the missing card:

No more hints are given for the remainder of the puzzles in this section. Good luck!

Puzzle 4

Here's a somewhat different type of puzzle. The suit symbols are distributed in the grid according to a system. Knowing this, what suit symbol is missing?

1	2	3	4	5	6
♠	♦	♣	♥	♠	♦
♣	**?**	♠	♦	♣	♥
♠	♦	♣	♥	♠	♦
♣	♥	♠	♦	♣	♥
♠	♦	♣	♥	♠	♦
♣	♥	♠	♦	♣	♥

Choose the missing symbol:

A.	B.	C.	D.
♥	♦	♣	♠

Puzzle 5

Four hands are dealt from a standard fifty-two-card deck to four different players, and each hand is laid out in a separate column as shown. In each of the hands there is the same pattern for you to unravel. Note that jacks have a value of 11, queens of 12, and kings of 13. Which card is missing from the fourth hand?

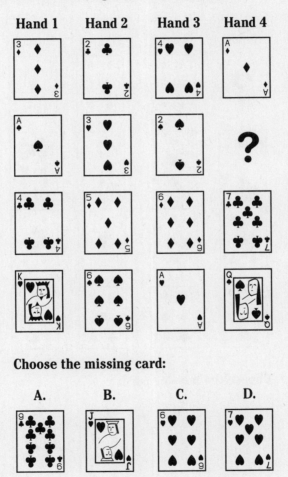

Hand 1   Hand 2   Hand 3   Hand 4

Choose the missing card:

A.   B.   C.   D.

Puzzle 6

As in previous puzzles, four hands are dealt from a standard fifty-two-card deck to four different players. Each hand is laid out in a separate column. Again, in each of the hands there is an identical pattern for you to discover. Which card is missing from the first hand? Note that jacks have a value of 11, queens of 12, and kings of 13.

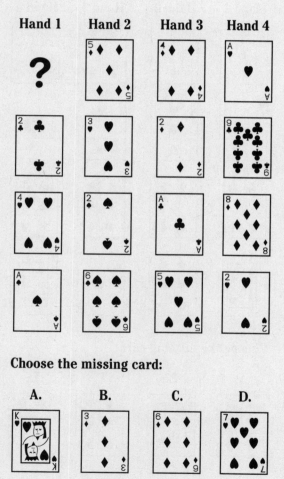

Choose the missing card:

Puzzle 7

Sixteen cards have been inserted in the following grid in a systematic way. Can you figure out how they have been inserted? If so, choose the missing card from the following options.

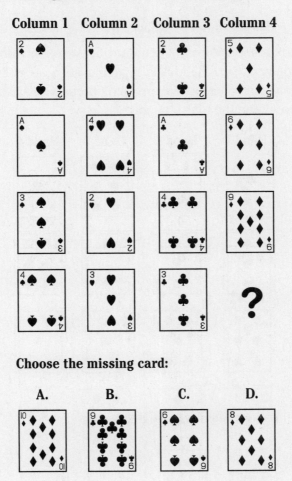

Choose the missing card:

A. B. C. D.

▸ DIFFICULT ◂

The three puzzles in this section are classified as "difficult" but if you have grasped the principles involved in solving the previous ones, it is merely a label.

Puzzle 8

Four hands are dealt from a standard fifty-two-card deck to four different players. Each hand is laid out in a separate column. Each hand reveals an identical pattern. Which cards are missing from the first hand and the fourth hand?

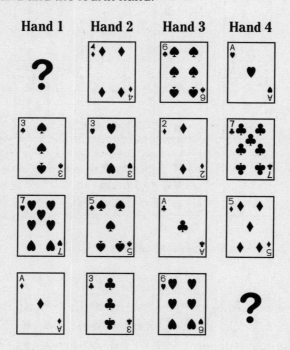

Choose the missing cards:

Hand 1

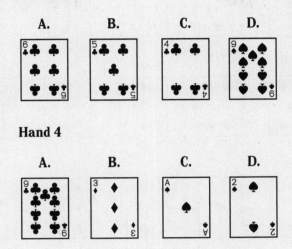

A.   **B.**   **C.**   **D.**

Hand 4

A.   **B.**   **C.**   **D.**

Puzzle 9

Three rows consisting of five cards each, drawn from the standard fifty-two-card deck, are laid out on a table as shown. Each row is built on the same pattern. Which card is missing from Row C? Note that jacks have a value of 11, queens of 12, and kings of 13.

Row A

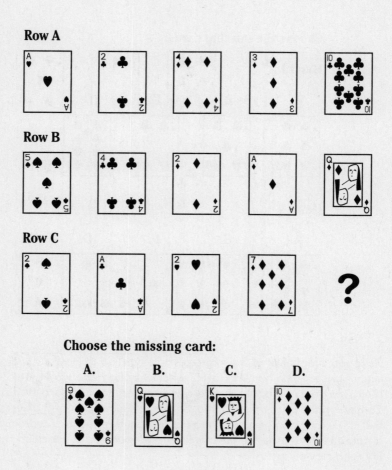

Row B

Row C

Choose the missing card:

A.   B.   C.   D.

Puzzle 10

This time, five rows consisting of five cards each are dealt on five different days. Here's how it is done. After Day 1, the deck is shuffled and a second row is laid out from the fifty-two-card deck. The same occurs for the remaining days. Photos are taken of the rows on each successive day. The photos are shown here. The rows are, surprisingly, connected in some specific way. Which card is missing from the row on Day 5?

Day 1

A♥ | 2♣ | 8♣ | 3♦ | 5♥

Day 2

5♥ | Q♠ | 7♣ | A♦ | J♥

Day 3

J♥ | 6♠ | 6♥ | 7♥ | 3♥

Day 4

3♥ | 4♣ | K♣ | A♠ | 9♦

Day 5

? | J♣ | A♣ | 2♥ | 7♦

Choose the missing card:

A. Q♥   B. 5♦   C. K♥   D. 9♦

The Odd Card Out

The puzzles in this section will test your ability to spot an intruder in a card arrangement. Specifically, you have to figure out what card or cards do not belong, or which column or row in an arrangement is nonsensical. Let's go through a simple example for illustrative purposes.

► ILLUSTRATION ◄

The cards in the following four columns were drawn from a standard fifty-two-card deck during a game of solitaire. But there is something that is impossible in the layout. Can you spot it?

Column 1   Column 2   Column 3   Column 4

Look at Columns 1 and 3 and you will see the same card—the four of clubs. This is impossible, because all the cards come from the same deck and there are no two cards of the same suit and numerical value in a deck. So the odd card out is one of the two four of clubs cards—your pick.

▶ EASY ◀

For the following three puzzles you will be given hints, just to get you warmed up for the harder puzzles.

Puzzle 11

Here's a solitaire layout. The cards in the four columns were drawn from a standard fifty-two-card deck. The rule used for playing this particular game of solitaire is the following: the cards drawn must be placed in decreasing value in each column from the top down, that is, from the largest at the top to the smallest at the bottom. One of the columns doesn't fit. Which one is it? **Hint:** keep your eyes on the values of the cards as you look at the cards in each column.

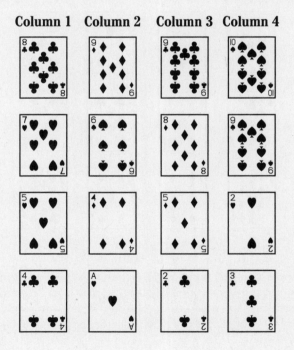

Column 1 Column 2 Column 3 Column 4

Puzzle 12

Here's a solitaire layout using the standard fifty-two-card deck. The rule this time is that the cards in a column must be in increasing order, from smallest at the top to largest at the bottom. Can you find the odd card out in the layout? **Hint:** in this version of solitaire, look for a card that has not been placed in a specific column according to the rule.

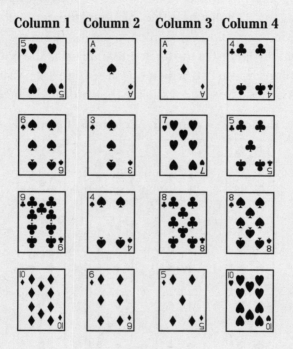

Column 1   Column 2   Column 3   Column 4

Most people think of tarot cards as part of ancient fortunetelling practices, but they were originally used to play ordinary card games in medieval Italy, spreading to Europe from there and much later to the rest of the world. The use of tarot cards for fortunetelling didn't start until the late 1700s.

Puzzle 13

One last solitaire puzzle! Note that there are only three columns this time. The game rule is also different. The cards must be laid out in a continuous fashion throughout the three columns: that is, the order of the cards in the second column continues the numerical order from the first, and the third from the second. Note: jacks have a numerical value of 11, queens of 12, and kings of 13. Two of the cards are out of order. Which ones? Again, the standard fifty-two-card deck is used. **Hint:** simply look for the cards that do not follow this rule.

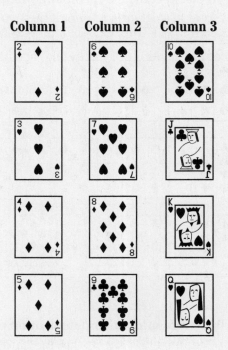

▶ MODERATELY HARD ◀

No more hints are given for the remainder of the puzzles in this section. You're on your own!

Puzzle 14

Ten cards are drawn from a standard deck by a card wizard. She lays them out in two rows, claiming that she produced two sequences that were not random in order to impress her audience. She then asked her audience to identify the pattern in each sequence. But an astute audience member noticed that she made a mistake, since one of the cards in one of the two sequences did not fit the "magical order." Which card is that? Note: jacks have a value of 11, queens of 12, kings of 13, and the ace has a value of 1.

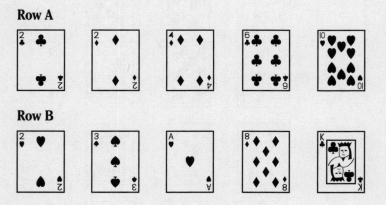

Puzzle 15

Five cards are drawn from a standard deck in no particular order. However, a close examination shows that the cards would form a logical sequence except for one that does not fit in, thus blocking the sequence from happening. Which card is that? Note that you will have to figure out the potential sequence first before identifying the culprit card. Again, jacks have a value of 11, queens of 12, and kings of 13.

Puzzle 16

Look at the following layout of cards. The cards have been distributed in a systematic fashion within the grid. But, somehow, one column does not fit in. Which one is it? Again, aces have a value of 1, jacks of 11, queens of 12, and kings of 13.

Column 1	Column 2	Column 3	Column 4	Column 5

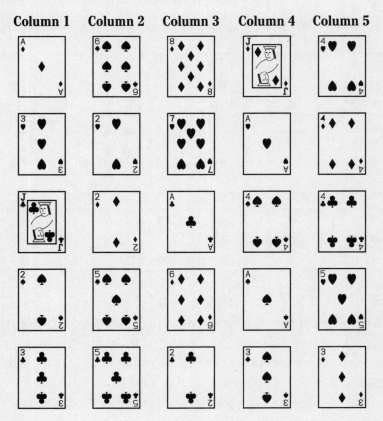

Puzzle 17

The cards in the following grid have been inserted in each column according to a rule. But by some error, one of the columns does not fit in with the other five. Which column is it? Obviously, you will have to figure out the insertion rule first before identifying the culprit column. Again, aces have a value of 1, jacks of 11, queens of 12, and kings of 13.

Column 1	Column 2	Column 3	Column 4	Column 5	Column 6

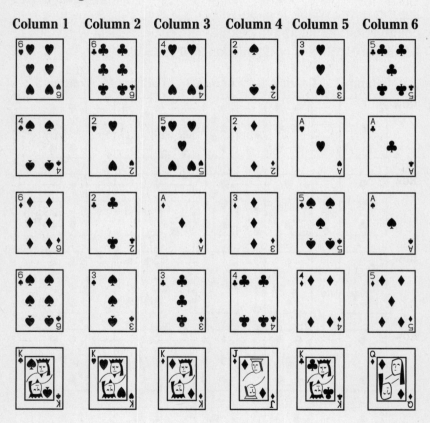

The three puzzles in this section provide a bit more of a challenge than the previous ones.

Puzzle 18

The cards in the grid have been inserted according to a rule. One of the rows does not fit in. Which row is it? Remember that aces have a value of 1, jacks of 11, queens of 12, and kings of 13.

Puzzle 19

Here's a layout of cards that reveals a specific arrangement. One of the cards does not fit in. Which one? Remember that aces have a value of 1, jacks of 11, queens of 12, and kings of 13.

Did you know that mathematicians have used playing cards systematically to develop probability theory? Here's an example of how cards can be used in this manner: how many different ways can four cards be drawn blindly from a standard deck? Can you figure out the answer?

Puzzle 20

Four rows of cards are dealt from a standard fifty-two-card deck. The cards in the rows are all connected by a pattern except for one. Which card does not fit in? Remember that aces have a value of 1, jacks of 11, queens of 12, and kings of 13.

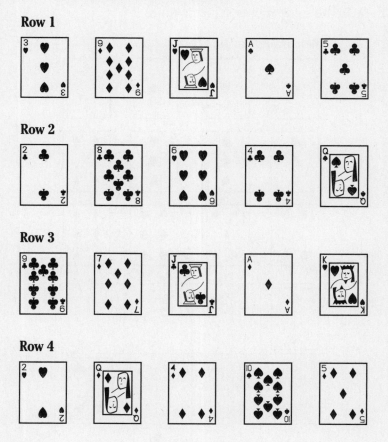

Row 1

Row 2

Row 3

Row 4

Card-Logic Mayhem

The five puzzles in this final section will challenge your card logic skills. Anything goes here. They vary in difficulty level, though. Some are harder than others. Good luck!

Puzzle 21

Four cards are placed in the following grid. Insert the remaining cards according to the following two rules: (1) each row and each column must have cards of all four suits (a heart, a club, a diamond, and a spade), and (2) no cards of the same number value can be in the same row or same column.

Remaining cards:

Puzzle 22

This time you have to place the nine given cards in the grid so that the values of the rows, columns, and two diagonals add up to the same constant sum. Three cards have been placed for you.

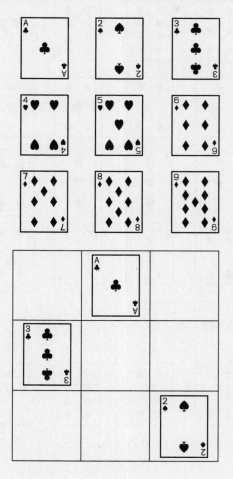

Puzzle 23

Sixteen cards are arranged in a grid according to a rule. What card is missing from this arrangement?

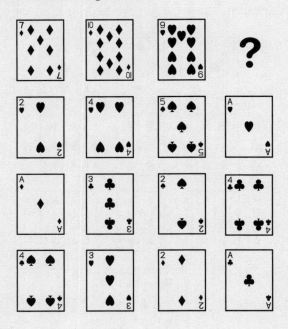

Choose the missing card:

A.   B.   C.   D.

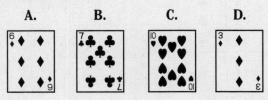

Puzzle 24

Place the following cards into the grid so that the value of the card on the bottom cell of the column equals the sum of the values of the three cards above it. Some of the cards have been put in the grid for you to get you started. Remember that the value of an ace is 1, a jack is 11, a queen is 12, and a king is 13.

Cards:

Puzzle 25

Fifteen cards are dealt, one after the other, from a standard fifty-two-card deck and laid out as shown. But something is not right. What is wrong?

Solitaire has become a very popular game in the computer age. There are thousands of online sites that allow you to play over 100 distinct solitaire games. Solitaire involves both luck and logic—a perfect combination!

CHAPTER 2

Doublets

Who in the world am I? Ah, that's the great puzzle.
—LEWIS CARROLL (1832–1898)

Most people know Lewis Carroll, the nom de plume of Charles Lutwidge Dodgson, as the writer of children's books, especially *Alice's Adventures in Wonderland* and *Through the Looking-Glass, and What Alice Found There*. It is perhaps not as well known that Carroll was one of the greatest puzzlemakers of all time, if not the greatest. One of Carroll's undisputed puzzle masterpieces is called the doublet. He created it for the magazine *Vanity Fair*, and the first doublet was published in the March 29, 1879, issue of the magazine. Carroll took the name for his puzzle from the witches' incantation in *Macbeth*: "Double, double, toil and trouble." The puzzle works at various levels—it requires knowledge of word meanings and an ability to see a connection between words and their spelling. Solving them requires a special kind of "word logic," as you will discover in this chapter. If you have never done doublets before, you're in for a true mental workout.

Basic Doublets

The basic doublet puzzle involves turning a word, given at the top of a "ladder," into another word, given at the bottom, by changing only one letter at a time, forming a genuine new word (not a proper name) with each letter change. The challenge is to do the transformation with the least number of word "links." You may find other solutions with more links, but the puzzles in this chapter require you to find the least number.

▶ ILLUSTRATION ◀

Let's go through the doublet puzzle introduced by Carroll himself: Turn HEAD into TAIL with four intervening links (words). Each link must consist of a legitimate word, excluding proper nouns, by changing one of the letters in the word above it. Note the semantic connection between "head" and "tail." Here's the solution, provided by Carroll himself:

HEAD
Link 1 ➡ heal
Link 2 ➡ teal
Link 3 ➡ tell
Link 4 ➡ tall
TAIL

Here's the breakdown of the steps involved.

HEAD
Step 1: change the "d" in "head" to "l" ➡ "heal"
Step 2: change the "h" in "heal" to "t" ➡ "teal"
Step 3: change the "a" in "teal" to "l" ➡ "tell"
Step 4: change the "e" in "tell" to "a" ➡ "tall"
Step 5: change the "l" in "tall" to "i" ➡ TAIL

Note that "Step 5" is equivalent to the final link. The word "step" is used here to describe the logical process.

In all doublets, no link can be a proper noun (such as a person's name, the name of a city, and so on) or an abbreviation.

Following are ten puzzles of this same basic type, organized from easy to difficult, which may be a matter of opinion. Veteran doublet solvers may find them all easy; others may find them all somewhat hard. Note that there may be more than one way to solve the doublets in this section. The possible ways are provided in the answers at the end of the book. Have fun!

▸ EASY ◂

These first puzzles should be fairly easy to solve, but they will get you in the right logical mindset for the tougher ones to come.

Puzzle 1

Turn LIFE into WORK with just three links. It certainly is true that "life" seems to be based on hard "work"!

LIFE

_____

_____

_____

WORK

Puzzle 2

Turn WHY into SUN with just three links. On a hot and humid day, you may indeed wonder "why" the "sun" is always beating down so hard!

WHY

_____

_____

_____

SUN

Puzzle 3

Turn SPY into WIN with just three links. No doubt that every "spy" wants to "win" the game of cat and mouse with the enemy!

SPY

_____

_____

_____

WIN

▸ MODERATELY HARD ◂

Puzzles 4 to 7 are classified as a bit harder than the previous ones, because the steps involved in producing the links are not as obvious. Good luck!

Puzzle 4

Turn FACE into PINK with just three links. Sometimes the cheeks on our "face" do seem to turn "pink."

FACE

_____

_____

_____

PINK

Carroll had initially named the doublets "word links," which he mentioned in a diary entry of March 12, 1878. In his pamphlet, *Word-links: A Game for Two Players, or a Round Game*, published in April 1878, he indicates that he invented the game for two girls to play on Christmas Day, 1877, because they usually "found nothing to do."

Puzzle 5

Turn GRADE into CRAZY with just two links. Getting good "grades" can often drive students "crazy," figuratively speaking, of course.

GRADE

_____

_____

CRAZY

Puzzle 6

Turn BLEND into GRIND with just three links. A good coffee "blend" results from a thorough "grind" of the beans, don't you agree?

BLEND

_____

_____

_____

GRIND

Puzzle 7

Turn WHILE into STARE with just three links. Every once in a "while" we all "stare," don't we?

WHILE

_____

_____

_____

STARE

▸ DIFFICULT ◂

The last three puzzles in this section will challenge your "doublet logic skills"!

Puzzle 8

Turn BLACK into CRAZE with just four links. Isn't "black" the latest "craze" in fashion?

BLACK

_____

_____

_____

_____

CRAZE

Puzzle 9

Turn LEAVE into TOAST with just four links. If you eat a big breakfast, you might have to "leave" some of your "toast," right?

LEAVE

_____

_____

_____

_____

TOAST

Given the popularity of the doublets published in *Vanity Fair*, in 1879 the publisher Macmillan put out a thirty-nine-page book containing several of the puzzles, titled *Doublets: A Word-Puzzle*. The book also became popular and was increased to seventy-three pages in a second edition, published in 1880. A third edition, put out in the same year, was enlarged to eighty-five pages. Doublets are still very popular today.

Puzzle 10

Turn GRAPE into SPINE with just five links. I'm not sure what the connection between "grape" and "spine" is. Is there one?

GRAPE

_____

_____

_____

_____

SPINE

Doublets Meet Anagrams

Carroll eventually modified the doublet game to make the puzzles more difficult. His new version involved the use of anagrams in one or more of the steps. An anagram in this case is defined as any word or words derived from a given word. For example, the letters of the word TOP can be rearranged to produce two other words: POT and OPT.

▶ ILLUSTRATION ◀

Here is the example Carroll himself used. It will serve to illustrate how to solve this type of challenging doublet puzzle.

Turn IRON into LEAD with six links. Each link must consist of a legitimate word, excluding proper nouns, either by changing one of the letters in the word above it or by rearranging the letters of the word above (called an "anagram step"). You may not do both in the same step.

IRON
Link 1→icon
Link 2→coin
Link 3→corn
Link 4→cord
Link 5→lord
Link 6→load
LEAD

Here's the breakdown of the steps involved.

IRON
Step 1: change the "r" in "iron" to "c" → "icon"
Step 2: rearrange the letters in "icon" (anagram step) → "coin"
Step 3: change the "i" in "coin" to "r" → "corn"
Step 4: change the "n" in "corn" to "d" → "cord"
Step 5: change the "c" in "cord" to "l" → "lord"
Step 6: change the "r" in "lord" to "a" → "load"
Step 7: change the "o" in "load" to "e" → LEAD

▸ EASY ◂

In the following three puzzles, there may be one anagram step.

Puzzle 11

Turn VEIL into DIME with just three links. It's impossible to buy a "veil," or anything else today, for just a "dime."

VEIL

_____

_____

_____

DIME

Puzzle 12

Turn READ into HAIR with just three links. Let's not "read" too much in people's "hair"styles.

READ

_____

_____

_____

HAIR

Puzzle 13

Turn PORE into LIPS with just three links. Hopefully we never get a "pore" on our "lips."

PORE

_____

_____

_____

LIPS

▸ **MODERATELY HARD** ◂

From now on there may be one or more anagram steps in the puzzles. Or there may be no anagram step at all!

Puzzle 14

Turn EVIL into NAME with just four links. Indeed, "evil" comes with many "names."

EVIL

_____

_____

_____

_____

NAME

Puzzle 15

Turn TRAP into SHOP with just three links. We all fall into the "trap" of "shopping" a bit too much, don't we?

TRAP

_____

_____

_____

SHOP

Puzzle 16

Turn LATE into REAP with just three links. Anyone who is "late" for something important may "reap" undesirable consequences.

LATE

_____

_____

_____

REAP

In his classic puzzle collection of 1965, *Language on Vacation*, Dmitri Borgmann renamed the doublet as the word ladder, which accurately describes the solution strategy itself, consisting of "word steps" that are connected logically as steps are on a real ladder.

Puzzle 17

Turn CHEAP into PANEL with just four links. Is there any connection between being "cheap" and a "panel"?

CHEAP

_____

_____

_____

_____

PANEL

▸ DIFFICULT ◂

The next three puzzles are a bit more challenging than the previous ones because they require trickier "steps."

Puzzle 18

Turn TRIAL into FROWN with just five links. Frivolous "trials" should certainly make you "frown."

TRIAL

_____

_____

_____

_____

_____

FROWN

The biologist John Maynard Smith once referred to the doublet in a scientific paper because he saw an analogy between the steps in doublets and the genetic instructions in chromosomes.

Puzzle 19

Turn MANE into LEAD with just three links. Certainly a good "mane" of hair can get some handsome actor the "lead" role.

MANE

_____

_____

LEAD

Puzzle 20

Turn BASS into RATE with just four links. How do you "rate" the "bass" in good songs?

BASS

_____

_____

_____

RATE

The deranged narrator of the novel *Pale Fire*, by Russian writer Vladimir Nabokov, recalls playing "word golf" (doublets) with a friend and boasts that some of his records are "hate-love in three, lass-male in four, and live-dead in five." (Can you find the solutions?)

Doublet Mayhem

The five puzzles in this final section will put your doublet logic skills to the test. Anything goes here. There may be one or more anagram steps or none. You will have to figure it out by yourself. Good luck! This time you will really need it.

Puzzle 21

Turn BRIDE into FREED with just three links. Does this doublet suggest that a "bride" is "freed" from her family at marriage? Does it imply that a "bride" might eventually seek to be "freed" from a bad marriage? Or both?

BRIDE

_____

_____

_____

FREED

Puzzle 22

Turn GRACE into LONER with just five links. There is little "grace" in being a "loner," so they say.

GRACE

_____

_____

_____

_____

_____

LONER

Puzzle 23

Turn BLAME into APPLE with just two links! Enough said!

BLAME

_____

_____

APPLE

Puzzle 24

Turn LEAD into RAIL with just four links. Some "railings" are made of "lead."

LEAD

_____

_____

_____

_____

RAIL

Puzzle 25

Turn TRAP into SLIP with three links. And be careful not to "slip" into any "trap."

TRAP

_____

_____

_____

SLIP

CHAPTER 3

Word Squares

False words are not only evil in themselves,
but they infect the soul with evil.
—SOCRATES (469–399 B.C.E.)

Placing words in a square arrangement so that the letters of the words will cross each other systematically within the square is a mental pursuit that has always fascinated us and seems to have held some mystical significance in the past. Word squares have been found in ancient cultures, constituting a spiritual form of writing called acrostic writing. In the Hebrew Bible, for example, the first four poems of the book of Lamentations are acrostics, the first part of the book of Nahum is an unfinished acrostic poem constructed with roughly half the letters of the Hebrew alphabet, the eighth section of the book of Proverbs is yet another twenty-two-line acrostic poem, and each eight-line stanza of Psalm 119 begins with a successive letter of the Hebrew alphabet. The latter is the oldest acrostic known.

Three-by-Three Squares

A three-by-three square, as the term suggests, is a square arrangement of three words consisting of three letters. The words are placed in the cells of corresponding rows and columns in such a way that their letters cross perfectly.

▸ ILLUSTRATION ◂

In the following puzzle, you are given three clues that correspond to the three words to be inserted in the rows and columns of the square figure.

CLUES

1. Opposite of "no"
2. Opposite of "girl"
3. A number that is more than zero but less than two

The answer to clue (1) is "yes." The answer to (2) is "boy." And the answer to (3) is "one." You will need to insert each in the cells of a row and corresponding column in such a way that the letters will cross perfectly with the other words. The only way to do this is shown here.

B	O	Y
O	N	E
Y	E	S

Just for the sake of completeness, notice that "boy" is placed in the cells of the top row and leftmost column; "one" is placed in the cells of the middle row and middle column; and "yes" is placed in the cells of the bottom row and rightmost column. Nice, right? These puzzles will test both your semantic and logical skills at once—you will need the former to solve the clues and the latter to insert the words accurately in the cells.

▸ EASY ◂

As usual, let's start off with five very easy puzzles, just to get you used to the genre.

Puzzle 1

CLUES
1. Opposite of "subtract"
2. Body of salt water
3. Opposite of "begin"

Puzzle 2

CLUES
1. A large mouse
2. A hot drink
3. A form of the verb "be"

Puzzle 3

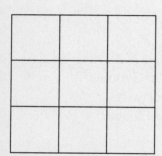

CLUES
1. Epoch
2. Past tense of "is"
3. Opposite of "old"

Puzzle 4

CLUES
1. Abbreviation of "Internet"
2. Supporter
3. A playing card

Puzzle 5

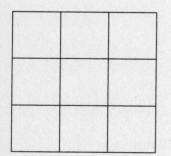

CLUES
1. Past tense of "get"
2. A cardinal number
3. A natural solid from which metal is extracted

▶ A LITTLE HARDER ◀

Now that you are used to this type of puzzle, it's time to make the puzzles a little harder.

Puzzle 6

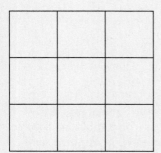

CLUES
1. Ovum
2. Generation
3. Open area of grassy land

Puzzle 7

CLUES
1. Chum
2. Allow
3. A type of beer

Puzzle 8

CLUES
1. Pigpen
2. A personal pronoun
3. The first even number

Puzzle 9

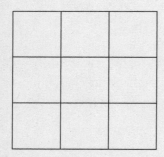

CLUES

1. Employ
2. A snakelike fish
3. Shade

Puzzle 10

CLUES

1. Past tense of "eat"
2. Dishonorable man
3. A wild animal's lair

A famous 5 x 5 word square, known as the Sator Square, was discovered by archaeologists in several ancient places—on a structure in the Roman city of Corinium (modern-day Cirencester), in England, and on a column in the city of Pompeii. The Latin words in the acrostic—*sator, arepo, tenet, opera, rotas*—form a palindrome and can be translated as "Arepo, the sower, carefully guides the wheels," which is believed to be a metaphor for "God controls the universe."

Four-by-Four Squares

A four-by-four square, as the term suggests, is a square arrangement of four words consisting of four letters. Just as in the previous puzzles, the objective is to identify the words by solving the clues and then placing them in the cells of the square so that their letters cross perfectly.

▸ MODERATELY HARD ◂

The four-by-four squares are a little harder than the previous three-by-three ones. Good luck!

Puzzle 11

CLUES

1. District
2. The polar type of this animal is white
3. Very young child
4. Lawn

Puzzle 12

CLUES

1. Care very much for someone
2. Egg-shaped
3. Animal fur
4. A sound that is made by dropping something into water

Puzzle 13

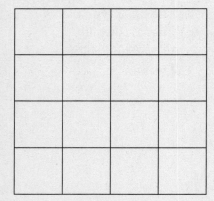

CLUES

1. Close by
2. Entice
3. Close-knit group
4. Region

Puzzle 14

CLUES

1. Impend
2. Too
3. Warning sign
4. Several

Lewis Carroll used an acrostic in a poem at the end of *Through the Looking-Glass*. When one takes the first letter of each line in the poem reading downward, it spells out the name of the girl that some say served as the inspiration for Carroll's Alice: Alice Pleasance Liddell.

Puzzle 15

CLUES
1. Jog
2. Opposite of "closed"
3. Portable shelter
4. Cord

▶ DIFFICULT ◀

The next few puzzles will turn the difficulty notch up a bit. Enjoy!

Puzzle 16

CLUES
1. A part of the eye
2. A bird's home
3. Unusual
4. Beam

Modern acrostic puzzles were created by Elizabeth Kingsley in the *Saturday Review* in March 1934. Kingsley called her puzzles double-crostics, and the completed grids revealed a famous quotation. In addition, the first letter of the answers could be used to form the title and author of a book, poem, or other written work.

Puzzle 17

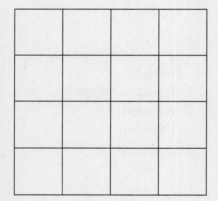

CLUES
1. Fluorescent lighting
2. To the inside
3. Burden
4. Soybean curd

Puzzle 18

CLUES
1. A small amount
2. Tool for holding objects firmly in place
3. Mix ingredients
4. Hearing organs

The Latin square is a square arrangement of given letters that do not necessarily make up words. The square was invented by the Swiss mathematician Leonhard Euler (1707–1783), because he saw in its layout many implications for logic and mathematics.

Puzzle 19

CLUES
1. Afresh
2. Said at the end of some prayers
3. Deceptive hockey move
4. Twentieth-century art and literary movement

Puzzle 20

CLUES
1. Legend
2. Steady movement of water
3. Opposite of "east"
4. Spheres

Five-by-Five Squares

The five puzzles in this final section will truly challenge your semantic and logical skills. The rules are the same. You are given five clues to identify the five words. Once you have done that, you will need to insert them in the square accurately. Good luck!

Puzzle 21

CLUES

1. A joint
2. Inexpensive
3. Strength
4. Unaccompanied
5. Opposite of "goodbye"

Puzzle 22

CLUES

1. Twelve
2. Object-locating device
3. Sexually excited
4. In front
5. Hawaiian greeting

Puzzle 23

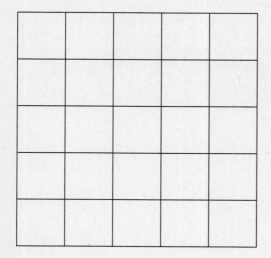

CLUES

1. Adored
2. Expunge
3. Musical drama
4. Corrupt
5. Lowland valleys

Puzzle 24

CLUES

1. Strong affection
2. Dish
3. Abrupt
4. Many "S" letters
5. Avows

Puzzle 25

CLUES
1. Type of farm
2. Location
3. Cut up
4. Rage
5. Tactless

Some people say that acrostic puzzles in particular help keep the brain strong and improve word fluency. By pulling words from the speech and language centers of your brain to complete the puzzles you are challenging your brain. Some experts believe that challenging your brain in this way may help stave off the onset of some diseases such as Alzheimer's.

CHAPTER 4

Word Logic Puzzles

*She had always wanted words; she loved them; grew up
on them. Words gave her clarity, brought reason, shape.*
—MICHAEL ONDAATJE (B. 1943)

Legend has it that the philosopher Parmenides (fifth century B.C.E.) invented logic as he sat on a cliff meditating. The ancient Greeks coined the word *lógos*, denoting both "word" and "reason." Clearly, they were keenly aware of the intrinsic connection between language and logic, coming up with the perfect term for it. Thus, the title "word logic" for this chapter is actually redundant—if something is a word, then it is logical. But it is a useful one for our purposes, nonetheless, because the goal here is to emphasize the connection between the two. In fact, you will be revisiting the same kinds of logic you used to solve the card puzzles in Chapter 1, employing words in place of cards. We may not be dealing with the great issues of logic and language here, but we can certainly have fun exploring the connection.

The Missing Word

The puzzles in this section are like the missing-card puzzles in Chapter 1. The difference is that you will have to identify the missing word rather than the missing card. Let's go through two together, just to get you started.

▶ ILLUSTRATION ◀

The missing word may be part of a system of meaning or it may be a word constructed according to some rule, or it may be something else entirely. Let's do an easy puzzle first.

A word is missing from the following set of words, all of which have something in common. Of the options given, which word fits into the set?

physics	chemistry	astronomy	?
zoology	botany	statistics	entomology

CHOOSE THE MISSING WORD:

A. geology
B. literature
C. philosophy
D. history

The words in the set all refer to sciences, as does option A (geology). The other three options do not.

Now let's do a puzzle of the "word construction" type. A word is missing from the following set of words that have something in common. Of the options given, which word is the correct one?

plop	?	did	mom
gig	fluff	kick	eve

CHOOSE THE MISSING WORD:

A. none
B. yes
C. wow
D. man

The common property is that all the words start and end with the same letter. So only the word in option C ("wow") has this property.

As you can see, you will really have to put on your thinking cap, since the common property could be anything.

▶ EASY ◀

For the following three puzzles, you are given hints just to get you warmed up for the harder puzzles.

Puzzle 1

The three words in the following set belong to a specific category. Of the options given, which word is the missing one? **Hint:** look for a meaning connection among the words.

knife	spoon	fork	plate
pan	masher	pot	bowl
oven	stove	broiler	?

CHOOSE THE MISSING WORD:

A. bed
B. car
C. platter
D. garage

Puzzle 2

A word is missing from the following set of words, all of which share a spelling pattern. Of the options given, which word is it? **Hint:** look for the type of letter with which a word ends.

see	data	arrive	too
idea	**?**	alumni	tree
panorama	love	plateau	into

CHOOSE THE MISSING WORD:
A. agenda
B. allow
C. enough
D. span

Puzzle 3

Here's another puzzle of the same kind. A word is missing from the following set of words, all of which share a common property. Of the options given, which word is it? **Hint:** again, look for a meaning pattern that allows you to group the words together.

?	mother	daughter	cousin
sister	brother	son	wife
aunt	grandmother	uncle	husband

CHOOSE THE MISSING WORD:
A. house
B. niece
C. job
D. school

▸ MODERATELY HARD ◂

No more hints are given for the remainder of the puzzles in this section. Good luck!

Puzzle 4

A word is missing from the following set of words, which are laid out in a specific way. Of the options given, which word is it?

altar	butter	cat	dog	ever
famous	grow	home	internet	just
knight	?	monster	no	opera
presume	quick	restroom	special	terrific
under	vouch	wonderful	xylophone	yes

CHOOSE THE MISSING WORD:
- A. west
- B. belong
- C. presumptuous
- D. lantern

Puzzle 5

A word is missing from the following set of words, which are placed in the columns according to a specific rule. Of the options given, which word is it?

Column 1	Column 2	Column 3	Column 4	Column 5
at	to	go	if	he
the	win	sin	buy	she
full	glow	sell	love	done
enter	train	spell	river	blend
simple	better	tingle	mantle	?

CHOOSE THE MISSING WORD:

A. secure

B. five

C. sober

D. till

The 2006 movie *Wordplay*, directed by Patrick Creadon, is a documentary dealing with our fascination with word games, focusing on Will Shortz, the *New York Times* puzzle editor. The movie tracks Shortz's lifelong interest in puzzles, concentrating on the crossword puzzle tournament he founded in 1978 and the enthusiasm it engenders in people from all walks of life.

Puzzle 6

Each column is organized in a systematic way. A word is missing from the second column. Of the options given, which word is it?

Column 1	Column 2	Column 3	Column 4	Column 5
car	church	jay	bathroom	baseball
bicycle	house	wren	kitchen	tennis
train	hotel	woodpecker	lounge	basketball
bus	cabin	dove	attic	soccer
vehicles	?	birds	rooms	sports

CHOOSE THE MISSING WORD:

A. subjects

B. ideas

C. buildings

D. stores

Puzzle 7

A word is missing from the following sequence of words, which are constructed and laid out according to a rule. Of the options given, which word is it?

enter	rest	trauma	allow
when	neat	trough	help
punk	knot	tank	?

CHOOSE THE MISSING WORD:

A. trip
B. knight
C. great
D. high

▸ DIFFICULT ◂

Now that you have become a pro at this, try these three more challenging puzzles!

Puzzle 8

A word is missing from the following set of words, all of which have something in common. Of the options given, which word is it?

Column 1	Column 2	Column 3	Column 4	Column 5
stop	live	meal	tale	parts
opts	veil	?	late	strap
pots	evil	lame	teal	traps

CHOOSE THE MISSING WORD:

A. male
B. mast
C. last
D. lake

Puzzle 9

A word is missing from Column 4. Each column is laid out according to a rule of construction. Of the options given, which word is the missing one?

Column 1	Column 2	Column 3	Column 4	Column 5
art	ton	pin	hum	sin
arts	tone	spin	?	sine
marts	stone	spine	chump	shine
smarts	stones	spines	chumps	shrine

CHOOSE THE MISSING WORD:

A. chore
B. humor
C. chum
D. home

Puzzle 10

The words in each column are arranged in a specific way. A word is missing from Column 2. Of the options given, which word is it?

Column 1	Column 2	Column 3	Column 4	Column 5
part	tall	send	brat	some
pant	tell	sent	beat	tome
pane	teal	seat	heat	tone
lane	meal	heat	heal	tune
line	?	heal	heel	dune

CHOOSE THE MISSING WORD:

A. must
B. team
C. tame
D. meat

The Odd Word Out

As in the case of the odd-card-out puzzles in Chapter 1, you will have to identify a word in a set that does not belong there. Let's do one together for illustrative purposes.

▶ ILLUSTRATION ◀

In the following layout of words, one does not fit in. Can you identify it?

Column 1	Column 2	Column 3	Column 4	Column 5
I (pronoun)	to	yes	cold	white
a (article)	in	pen	true	loved
a (same article)	so	hot	best	jester
I (same pronoun)	we	job	wins	river

Did you see the pattern? The words in Column 1 are written with one letter, those in Column 2 with two, those in Column 3 with three, those in Column 4 with four, and those in Column 5 with five. The word that does not fit into this pattern is "jester," which is in Column 5 but has six letters, not five.

▶ EASY ◀

For the first three puzzles below, you are given hints to get you warmed up for the harder puzzles.

Puzzle 11

Except for one, the words in the following set share a common property. Can you identify the odd word out? **Hint:** the words can be grouped together into a category.

lake	river	ocean	shore
pond	stream	sea	bay
gulf	lagoon	creek	brook

Puzzle 12

The words in the following set share a common pattern. One does not fit in. Can you identify it? **Hint:** look for a spelling peculiarity.

moon	week	soon	deem
radii	aardvark	mean	agree
vacuum	bloom	bazaar	coffee

Puzzle 13

The words in the following set share a common pattern. One does not fit in. Can you identify it? **Hint:** look for a similar kind of spelling peculiarity to the previous puzzle.

better	winner	rudder	doodle
arrow	bass	will	glimmer
little	pizza	accrue	egg

▶ MODERATELY HARD ◀

No more hints are given for the remainder of the puzzles in this section. Good luck!

Puzzle 14

Each column of the grid displays a specific pattern. This is broken in one of the columns because one of its words does not fit in. Can you identify that word?

Column 1	Column 2	Column 3	Column 4	Column 5
black	circle	jazz	ear	shirt
white	square	symphony	nose	pants
red	triangle	blues	arm	dress
blue	rectangle	rap	mouth	neck
green	ellipse	concerto	leg	jacket

Puzzle 15

Each column of the grid displays a specific pattern. This is broken in one of the columns because one of its words does not fit in. Can you identify the culprit word?

Column 1	Column 2	Column 3	Column 4	Column 5
true	must	aroma	built	band
blue	tryst	panorama	guilt	trend
sue	best	media	melt	demand
glue	chest	stigma	belt	friend
rue	toast	enigma	vault	found

Puzzle 16

The words in each pair within a column are connected in a specific way. However, one of the pairs does not fit in. Can you identify the pair?

Column 1	Column 2	Column 3	Column 4	Column 5
tips	not	meet	keep	trip
spit	ton	teem	peek	pert

The Austrian philosopher Ludwig Wittgenstein (1889–1951) once wrote: "For a large class of cases—though not for all—in which we employ the word 'meaning' it can be defined thus: the meaning of a word is its use in the language."

Puzzle 17

Each column of the grid displays a specific pattern. This is broken in one of the columns because one of its words does not fit in. Can you identify the culprit word?

Column 1	Column 2	Column 3	Column 4	Column 5
ripe	well	try	climb	love
rise	tell	cry	clime	live
wise	tall	coy	crime	life
wine	talk	boy	prime	wise

▸ DIFFICULT ◂

It's time to turn the difficulty level up a few notches. Enjoy!

Puzzle 18

Each of the rows, except one, involves a pattern. Which row is the culprit one?

Row 1	base	ball	park
Row 2	ship	yard	stick
Row 3	war	fare	well
Row 4	spin	off	shoot
Row 5	worth	while	like

The great British puzzlemaker Henry E. Dudeney (1857–1930) claimed that: "The history of puzzles entails nothing short of the actual story of the beginnings and development of exact thinking in man."

Puzzle 19

The words in each column are constructed in a certain way, but one does not fit in. Can you identify it?

Column 1	Column 2	Column 3	Column 4	Column 5
rough	friend	crime	shell	always
rug	fiend	mice	hell	sway
hug	dine	rice	she	away
our	ride	ice	heck	sly
hog	den	mire	sell	alas

Puzzle 20

The words in each column are inserted according to a theme. One does not fit in. Can you identify it?

Column 1	Column 2	Column 3	Column 4	Column 5
gloves	addition	tie	atom	radio
stick	subtraction	scarf	molecule	television
helmet	exponents	hat	electron	print
puck	fractions	glut	proton	digital
hockey	mathematics	fashion	matter	media

Word-Logic Mayhem

The five puzzles in this final section vary in difficulty level. Actually, at this point in the chapter, you might find these to be rather easy. Have fun!

Puzzle 21

Insert the following words into the grid in such a way that no two letters (in any of the words) occur in the same row or the same column. That is, if a word has an "s" in it, then that letter cannot occur in any of the words in the row or column where the word occurs. Three of the words are inserted for you.

smart, see, suck, now, new, nib, pill, puck, pep

	puck	
now		
		pep

Puzzle 22

The words in each row display a specific pattern. Figure out the pattern and then choose which word is missing from the fifth row.

Row 1	all	cat	ball	and	act
Row 2	me	sell	best	neck	jest
Row 3	in	sin	flint	irk	chin
Row 4	on	son	bond	most	shock
Row 5	sun	punt	lust	?	trust

CHOOSE THE MISSING WORD:

A. run

B. fin

C. art

D. mop

Puzzle 23

The words in each row display a specific pattern, different from the previous puzzle. Figure out the pattern and then choose which word is missing from the fifth row.

Row 1	blurb	baby	lobby	bomb	bamboozle
Row 2	tall	level	lonely	lately	linoleum
Row 3	buffer	fifth	fiefdom	affair	firefly
Row 4	bass	system	sustain	sash	sister
Row 5	mom	?	mime	medium	meme

CHOOSE THE MISSING WORD:

A. ladder

B. simmer

C. cactus

D. fandom

Puzzle 24

Let's do one more like the previous two. The words in each row display a pattern, different from the previous puzzles. Figure out the pattern and then choose which word is missing from the fifth row.

Row 1	crime	crack	cranberry	critique	crab
Row 2	prime	print	prank	prism	proof
Row 3	great	grow	green	grass	grape
Row 4	trip	train	truck	trust	trick
Row 5	frill	frustrate	frost	fruit	?

CHOOSE THE MISSING WORD:

A. funny

B. flip

C. frank

D. fishy

Puzzle 25

The words in each column display a specific pattern. Figure out the pattern and then choose which word is missing from the fifth column.

Column 1	Column 2	Column 3	Column 4	Column 5
ankle	amplify	ant	arcane	awry
ball	bake	bark	blend	busy
can	carry	cling	crest	?
dove	deed	destiny	dry	dinner
effort	easy	entrance	evolve	enormous

CHOOSE THE MISSING WORD:

A. art

B. dime

C. erase

D. correct

The topic of logic raises a key question: Can anyone develop logic skills? In short, yes. The brain is like most of the muscles in your body; it requires exercise and stimulation. Contemplating and deciphering puzzles (or other games that require reasoning skills) are good ways to exercise your brain and make it sharper.

CHAPTER 5

Logical Deductions

A good puzzle, like virtue, is its own reward.
—HENRY E. DUDENEY (1857–1930)

We all love stories in which a master detective, like Sherlock Holmes, uses ingenious logic to solve crimes, drawing a conclusion from clues. Known as deductive logic, this concept goes back to the ancient Greeks, especially Aristotle, who called it "syllogistic" reasoning, whereby you are led to one and only one conclusion on the basis of given premises. Thus, if it is agreed that all human beings have one head and that Charlotte is a human being, then it can be logically concluded that Charlotte also has one head. The puzzles in this chapter require only logical deduction to solve. They involve no play on words, no guessing, no technical know-how—just reasoning like the great fictional detectives, drawing inferences and reaching the only possible conclusion from the given facts. Common-sense knowledge is, of course, required—for example, a mother is older than her children, an only child has no brothers or sisters, and so on.

Deduction Puzzles

The genre of puzzles in this section was invented by the British puzzlemaker Henry Dudeney, who along with Lewis Carroll (Chapter 2) and the American Sam Loyd (1841–1911) is considered to be one of the greatest puzzlemakers of all time. These puzzles require you to deduce who is what: Is Alex the lawyer? Is Sarah the engineer? In other words, you will have to figure out how two or more sets of facts relate to each other: What first name belongs with which last name? What jobs do certain persons do? And so on.

▶ ILLUSTRATION ◀

Let's go through a paraphrase of one of Dudeney's original puzzles in this genre. If you have never done these before, it is useful to read completely through the illustration.

> *Basel, Julia, and Sarah work for the same company. One is the director, another the engineer, and another is the accountant, but not necessarily in that order. The accountant is an only child and earns the least. Sarah married Basel's brother. She earns more than the engineer. What position does each person fill?*

To solve this puzzle methodically, a cell chart, such as the following, might help. It will allow you to keep track of the various deductions you make along the way to a solution.

	Director	Accountant	Engineer
Basel			
Julia			
Sarah			

If you conclude, for instance, that one of the three people cannot be the director, then put an ✖ in the cell opposite the person's name under the column Director. If you deduce that one of the three is the engineer, then put a different mark opposite that person's name under the column headed Engineer, eliminating the remaining cells in the column (since there can be only one engineer) with ✖s. The solution is complete when you have placed exactly one mark in each row and column.

Let's start. We are told that "the accountant is an only child" and that "Sarah married Basel's brother." Aha—Basel has a brother. So Basel is not an only child, right? So by exclusion, he cannot be the accountant. Why? Because the accountant is an only child, and Basel is not. So we can exclude him as the accountant:

	Director	Accountant	Engineer
Basel		✖	
Julia			
Sarah			

Next, we are told that Sarah "earns more than the engineer." Clearly, she is not the person who earns the least, which is the case for the accountant. What do we conclude? Well, if the accountant earns the least and Sarah does not, then she is not the accountant. We can now eliminate her as the accountant too:

	Director	Accountant	Engineer
Basel		✖	
Julia			
Sarah		✖	

Since Basel and Sarah are not the accountant, this leaves Julia as filling that position, as the empty cell in the chart also makes clear. So we put a dot in that cell and exclude all other possibilities for Julia, of course. If she's the accountant, she cannot be anything else. We show this as follows:

	Director	Accountant	Engineer
Basel		✖	
Julia	✖	•	✖
Sarah		✖	

Let's go back to the statement that Sarah "earns more than the engineer." What can we deduce from this? Well, she cannot be the engineer, since she earns more than whomever that person is. So we can eliminate this possibility for Sarah:

	Director	Accountant	Engineer
Basel		✖	
Julia	✖	•	✖
Sarah		✖	✖

As we can now see, the only possibility for the engineer is Basel. We put a dot in the appropriate cell and add ✖ for the Director cell.

	Director	Accountant	Engineer
Basel	✖	✖	•
Julia	✖	•	✖
Sarah		✖	✖

The only cell left for Sarah is under Director. That's who she is.

	Director	Accountant	Engineer
Basel	✖	✖	•
Julia	✖	•	✖
Sarah	•	✖	✖

To summarize: Basel is the engineer, Julia the accountant, and Sarah the director. Neat, right? You may not need charts as you go through the puzzles—many puzzle solvers can deduce everything in their head. But there is a chart after each puzzle for the sake of convenience.

▸ EASY ◂

So that you can become familiar with the type of reasoning involved in solving this type of puzzle, here are three easy ones.

Puzzle 1

Three women, Ms. White, Ms. Black, and Ms. Gray, went out to dinner at a trendy restaurant. One wore a white dress, one a black dress, and one a gray dress. The colors of the dresses and the names of the women did not match. Ms. Black sat next to someone who wore a gray dress. What dress color was each woman wearing?

	White dress	Black dress	Gray dress
Ms. White			
Ms. Black			
Ms. Gray			

Puzzle 2

Mr. Chan, Mr. Darrow, and Mr. Farrar work as a programmer, designer, and analyst, but not necessarily in that order. On the basis of the given clues, what is each man's occupation?

1. Mr. Farrar makes more money than the programmer.
2. Mr. Darrow gets along well with the programmer.
3. The analyst earns the least.

	Mr. Chan	Mr. Darrow	Mr. Farrar
Programmer			
Designer			
Analyst			

Puzzle 3

In a certain family, the father, mother, son, and daughter are called by their nicknames—Bo, Jo, Spy, and Geek—but not necessarily in that order. Geek is older than the father. Bo is younger than his sister. Jo is a female. How are the four related to each other?

	Father	Mother	Son	Daughter
Bo				
Jo				
Spy				
Geek				

▸ MODERATELY HARD ◂

It's time to move on to harder puzzles!

Puzzle 4

Bertha, Paula, Rhonda, and Sheila are musicians. One is a drummer, one a pianist, one a singer, and one a guitarist, though not necessarily in that order. Bertha and Paula attended the singer's debut with the hottest band in town the other night. Paula, the guitarist, and the pianist are good friends. The pianist performs often with Bertha and Rhonda. Who is the singer, and who plays which instrument?

	Drummer	Pianist	Singer	Guitarist
Bertha				
Paula				
Rhonda				
Sheila				

The great fictional detectives excelled at deductive logic. The first one was Edgar Allan Poe's C. Auguste Dupin, who appeared in April 1841, when *Graham's Magazine* published Poe's classic mystery story "The Murders in the Rue Morgue." Following Poe, Sir Arthur Conan Doyle created Sherlock Holmes, who became a household name, amazing his readers by explaining his reasoning at the end of each story.

Puzzle 5

Six scientists—five women and one man—participated at a climate change conference last year. On the basis of the clues provided, can you determine the scientific profession of each one—geophysicist, mathematician, computer scientist, chemist, biologist, and anthropologist?

1. Kayla, Lauren, Jane, and the mathematician are colleagues at MIT.
2. Paul, the only male in the group, teaches at Princeton.
3. Maria teaches at Princeton.
4. The biologist is a female.
5. At the end of the conference, some of the experts had dinner together. Sitting around the table were the computer scientist, Jane, the anthropologist, the chemist, and Paul.
6. Kayla attended a session with the anthropologist and the chemist.
7. Lauren is a good friend of the anthropologist.

	Geo	Math	Computer	Chem	Biology	Anthro
Kayla						
Lauren						
Paul						
Maria						
Jane						
Patricia						

Puzzle 6

Six married couples decided to go out to dinner together last week. Can you match the couples by name on the basis of the following clues?

1. The male partners are named Alex, Ben, Chuck, Dick, Everett, and Frank.
2. The female partners are named Ashley, Barb, Charlotte, Debbie, Emma, and Fiona.
3. The names of each partner in a couple do not start with the same letter.
4. No two married partners sat next to each other.
5. Ashley sat next to Ben on her left and Chuck on her right.
6. Ashley's husband goes bowling every weekend with Everett and Frank.
7. Alex sat next to Barb on his left and Charlotte on his right.
8. Alex's wife frequently plays tennis with Emma and Fiona.
9. Chuck's wife plays golf with Barb and Fiona.
10. Fiona is not married to Ben.

	Ashley	Barb	Charlotte	Debbie	Emma	Fiona
Alex						
Ben						
Chuck						
Dick						
Everett						
Frank						

Puzzle 7

Mr. Crimson Sr., Mr. Maroon Sr., and Mr. Scarlet Sr. live near each other. Each man has a son, Mr. Crimson Jr., Mr. Maroon Jr., and Mr. Scarlet Jr. On the basis of the given clues, determine what color tie each father and each son wears.

1. The fathers always wear a crimson, maroon, and scarlet tie, but none wear the color of tie corresponding to his name.
2. The sons also always wear a crimson, maroon, and scarlet tie, but again, none wear the color of tie corresponding to his name.
3. No son wears the same color tie as his father.
4. Mr. Maroon Sr. does not wear a crimson tie.

	Mr. Crimson Sr.	Mr. Maroon Sr.	Mr. Scarlet Sr.
Crimson			
Maroon			
Scarlet			
	Mr. Crimson Jr.	Mr. Maroon Jr.	Mr. Scarlet Jr.
Crimson			
Maroon			
Scarlet			

▶ DIFFICULT ◀

For the remaining three puzzles in this section, you will have to connect three sets of variables—for example, names, jobs, and ages. This raises the difficulty level considerably. Appropriate charts are provided for you.

Puzzle 8

Five children go swimming together every Sunday. The children are three, four, five, six, and seven years of age. Can you determine the full names (first and last) and ages of the children on the basis of the given clues?

1. Tina's mother is not Mrs. Blue or Mrs. Green.
2. Tina is neither the youngest nor the oldest child.
3. Tina is one-year older than Len but one-year younger than some other child.
4. The Brown child is older than Tina.
5. Three of the children are Tina, the White child, and the four-year-old.
6. Len is not the Green child.
7. Laura's mother is neither Mrs. White nor Mrs. Green.
8. Laura is not the youngest or the oldest.
9. Rita is not the oldest.
10. The White child is the youngest.
11. One of the children is named Glen.

		Last Names					Ages				
		Gray	White	Green	Brown	Blue	3	4	5	6	7
Names	Tina										
	Len										
	Laura										
	Rita										
	Glen										

Puzzle 9

Becky, Chris, Dean, Inez, and Mark were at a new café yesterday, trying out its coffee menu. Each was wearing a different color shirt (black, blue, green, white, red), and each one ordered a different type of coffee (espresso, cappuccino, latte, Americano, regular). On the basis of the given clues, what color shirt did each person wear, and what beverage did each one order?

1. Becky did not wear black or blue.
2. Chris ordered the regular coffee.
3. Chris did not wear the black or blue shirt.
4. Three of the friends, Chris, Inez, and the one who wore white, got into an argument over which was the best coffee.
5. Becky did not order cappuccino.
6. Dean ordered espresso.
7. Inez ordered Americano.
8. The person who ordered cappuccino wore black.
9. The person who ordered espresso wore red.

Names	Shirt Color					Coffee				
	Black	Blue	Green	White	Red	Espresso	Cappuccino	Latte	Americano	Regular
Becky										
Chris										
Dean										
Inez										
Mark										

Puzzle 10

Andy, Barb, Fran, Rose, and Sam work at an amusement park. Their surnames (last names) are, in no particular order, Cash, Dane, Mill, Smith, and Wills. Each person sells only one kind of fare—candy, ice cream, peanuts, popcorn, and nachos. From the following clues, determine each person's full name and the type of refreshment he or she sells.

1. Andy, the Mill vendor, and the ice cream vendor always work overtime.
2. Barb sells popcorn.
3. Andy does not sell peanuts or nachos.
4. The candy vendor is surnamed Smith.
5. Barb is a good friend of both the Cash and Dane vendors.
6. Wills does not sell popcorn.
7. Fran is a good friend of the Dane and Wills vendors.
8. The Cash vendor sells peanuts.
9. Rose is not related to the Wills vendor.
10. The Dane vendor sells ice cream.

G.K. Chesterton's Father Brown, a priest-detective, and Agatha Christie's Hercule Poirot, a dapper detective, also use the same kind of logic of Dupin and Holmes to solve crimes.

Names	Last Names					Refreshments				
	Cash	Dane	Mill	Smith	Wills	candy	ice cream	peanuts	popcorn	nachos
Andy										
Barb										
Fran										
Rose										
Sam										

Truth Tellers and Liars

The British puzzlemaker Hubert Phillips (1891–1964) invented an ingenious deduction puzzle that has become a classic in this genre. It goes under several names—the name used here is Truth Tellers and Liars. Solving it requires clear, logical thinking, even though sometimes you might think that there is no way to figure out the truth of the matter. If you have never done these, they might all seem challenging at first. You will find out, however, that some are easier than others. They are all a lot of fun to do!

▶ ILLUSTRATION ◀

Let's go through a paraphrase of one of Phillips's original puzzles.

The members of a pristine island culture belong to one of two clans—the Baus or the Maus. It is known that the members of the Bau clan always tell the truth, whereas the members of the Mau clan always lie—no exceptions. A visitor to the island, intrigued by its wonderful social system and many dialects, came across three island natives.

"To which clan do you belong?" the visitor asked the first individual.

"Dran," replied the individual in his native dialect, inferring what the visitor asked, even though he did not know English.

"What did he say?" asked the visitor of the second and third individuals, both of whom spoke English.

"He said, 'I am a Bau,'" claimed the second.

"No, he said, 'I am a Mau,'" claimed the third.

On the basis of the last two answers, can you determine to which clan the two individuals belonged? Is it possible to determine the clan membership of the first individual?

Solving this type of puzzle involves setting up hypothetical situations and then reasoning about their logical implications. Let's do so with the statement by the first individual—"Dran." If the individual were a member of the truth-telling Bau clan, he would say so. A Bau always tells the truth. So "Dran" can be translated as "I am a Bau." Let's consider the other possibility, namely, that the individual was a member of the mendacious Mau clan. Being a liar, he would never admit that he was a Mau, since that would be the truth. So as a liar, he would also say, "I am a Bau." Either way, we have just figured out that the first individual's statement has to be "I am a Bau," no matter what clan he belonged to.

The second individual said it like it is. As we just found out, the first individual had indeed said "I am a Bau" (true or false). So the second individual is definitely a member of the Bau clan. The third individual clearly lied. The first individual did not say "I am a Mau." So from this we can deduce that he is, in fact, a member of the Mau clan.

Needless to say, it is not possible to determine the clan to which the first member belonged.

▸ EASY ◂

For each of the ten puzzles in this section, members of the Baus always tell the truth and members of the Maus always lie.

Puzzle 11

The visitor in the previous illustrative puzzle next came across two other individuals who spoke a different dialect. The visitor asked the first one, who understands but does not speak English: "Are you a Bau?" He answered: "Gur." He asked the second one, a woman who spoke perfect English: "What did he say?" "He said, 'No, I am a Mau,'" claimed the woman. Can you figure out the clan to which she belonged?

Puzzle 12

The visitor then came across three other individuals—two women and a man—who spoke yet another dialect. She asked the women the following question: "Are you a Bau or a Mau?" Neither woman spoke English, although they figured out the visitor's question intuitively. The first one answered "Muma," and the second one also answered "Muma." The man, who spoke English, intervened and said: "They said they are both Baus, but they lied." Can you figure out to which clans the three belonged?

Puzzle 13

The same visitor went to another part of the island and ran into three more individuals, A, B, and C, who spoke yet another different dialect in this multilingual society. This time she asked A and B the same question: "Do you belong to the same clan?" The responses were as follows:

Individual A: "Yes."
Individual B: "Yes."
She then asked C: "Did A and B tell the truth?"
His answer was:
Individual C: "No."
To which clan did each one belong?

▶ MODERATELY HARD ◀

You are now ready to move on to harder puzzles.

Puzzle 14

The visitor met four other individuals, consisting of two married couples—A, a male, is married to B, a female; and C, a male, is married to D, a female. Clan members can and often do intermarry—Baus with Maus. The visitor was told that B is a Bau. They made the following statements to the visitor:

Individual A: "I am a Bau."
Individual B: "Yes, my husband is a Bau."
Individual C: "A lied, he's a Mau."
Individual D: "My husband told you the truth."
Can you identify the clan to which each one belongs?

Puzzle 15

The visitor ran into two other couples from yet another part of the island. They too spoke some English. She asked A and B, "Do you belong to the Baus?" Here are their answers in their native dialect:

Individual A: "Uma."
Individual B: "Uma."
The visitor then asked C and D, who spoke English: "What clan did A and B say they belonged to?"
Individual C: "The Baus, and it's the truth."
Individual D: "No, they said they belonged to the Maus."
To which clan did each one belong?

Puzzle 16

The visitor ran into yet another pair of couples—A (husband) and B (wife), and C (husband) and D (wife). The visitor was told beforehand that the members of each couple belonged to the different clans—each couple consisted of a Bau and a Mau. She asked A and B: "What clan do you belong to?"

Individual A: "Zina."
Individual B: "Zina."
She then asked the other couple: "What did A say?"
Individual C: "He said that he was a Bau, and that's the truth."
Individual D: "He said he was a Mau."
What clan do each of these individuals belong to?

Puzzle 17

The visitor ran into yet another pair of couples—A is married to B, and C to D. She knows beforehand that only one of them is a Mau; the other three are Baus. Knowing this, she employs trick logic by asking A: "Are you a Bau?" He answered:

Individual A: "Yes, I am."
Here's what the others had to say:
Individual B: "A is indeed a Bau."
Individual C: "No, A and B are liars. Only I am a Bau."
Individual D: "I am a Bau."
Can you identify the Mau in the group?

This puzzle genre, as mentioned, was invented by Hubert Phillips who also devised many other ingenious puzzles in the 1930s under the pseudonym "Caliban" for the *Nation* and the *New Statesman*. That name comes from the monstrous personage in Shakespeare's play *The Tempest*, clearly alluding to the monstrously difficult puzzles Phillips concocted.

▶ DIFFICULT ◀

The next three puzzles will truly challenge your logic skills. Good luck!

Puzzle 18

The island visitor met three brothers and three sisters—all from the Bau clan except one, who moved away a while back to marry someone from the Mau clan and became a liar. We will call them Brothers A, B, C and Sisters A, B, C. Here's what they said.

> *Brother A: One of the sisters is the odd one out; she went over to the Maus, becoming an instant liar.*
> *Sister A: No, one of the brothers is the odd one out; he is the one who went over to the Maus, becoming an instant liar.*
> *Brother B: I am a Bau.*
> *Sister B: I, too, am a Bau.*
> *Brother C: Brother A is a liar.*
> *Sister C: Brother C told you the truth.*
> Can you identify the individual who belongs to the Maus?

Puzzle 19

This time, the visitor came across three people, who were obviously friends. She asked one of the individuals: "Are your two friends both Maus?" The person answered as follows:

> *Individual A: "They are."*
> *So she asked the other two: "Did your friend tell the truth?"*
> *Individual B: "He did."*
> *Individual C: "He didn't."*
> Can you determine to which clans the three individuals belong?

Puzzle 20

The visitor decided to visit one last clan, where yet another dialect is spoken. She meets a female, Individual A, and two males, Individuals B and C. She asks A, "Are you a Bau?" She receives the following answer in A's native dialect:

Individual A: "Suna."
The visitor then asks B and C: "What did she say?"
Here are their answers:
Individual B: "She said 'no.'"
Individual C: "She did not say 'no,' because she is a Bau."
Can you figure out to which clan each individual belongs?

Drawing-Out Logic

There is another type of puzzle genre, here called Drawing-Out Logic, that involves a similar type of deductive reasoning. You will be asked to determine how many draws are needed to get a pair of billiard balls or socks that match in color from a box of differently colored balls or socks. That's all there is to it. Let's do an illustrative one together.

▶ ILLUSTRATION ◀

Let's start with the classic puzzle in the genre. By the way, no one really knows for sure who the inventor of these puzzles was.

In a box there are ten billiard balls, five white and five black. They are all the same, except for the color. With a blindfold on, what is the least number of balls you must draw out in order to be sure to get a pair of balls—two white balls or two black balls—that matches?

The answer is three! Follow the reasoning. Let's say you pull out a white ball first. If you are lucky, your second draw will produce another white ball. All you needed were two draws. But you cannot assume fortune, because you are required to be sure, not lucky, that the balls match.

So assume the worst-case scenario. You draw out a white ball. Your second draw produces a black ball. Now you have a white and a black in hand. Go back and draw out a third ball. That ball will be either white or black, of course. If it is white, it matches the white ball you already have in your hand. If it is black, it matches the black ball you have in your hand. Either way, that third ball will produce a color match.

The order of the draws does not change this. You could draw out a black ball first and a white ball second. The third ball will match the color of one or the other.

Puzzle 21

Let's make a slight change to the illustrative puzzle. The box contains five white billiard balls and five black billiard balls. How many balls must you draw out, with a blindfold on, in order to be sure (not lucky) to get two black ones?

Puzzle 22

Let's make things a little more complicated. This time there are twenty-five balls in the box—five white, five black, five red, five green, and five blue. With a blindfold on, again, what is the least number of balls you must draw out in order to be sure to get a pair of balls that matches—two white, two black, two red, two green, or two blue?

Puzzle 23

Let's do another version. The box has the same twenty-five balls—five white, five black, five red, five green, and five blue. With a blindfold on, what is the least number of balls you must draw out in order to be sure to get a pair of red balls?

Puzzle 24

Let's do one more puzzle with the twenty-five balls—five white, five black, five red, five green, and five blue. With a blindfold on, again, what is the least number of balls you must draw out in order to be sure to get all five blue balls?

Puzzle 25

Let's switch to socks in the box. Be careful! A pair of socks has a left (foot) and a right (foot) sock. There are ten socks in the box, all the same color. Five are for the left foot and five for the right foot. You are asked to draw out a pair of socks—consisting of a left-footed and a right-footed sock. How many draws will you need in order to be sure that you get such a pair?

Henry Dudeney provides one of the most penetrating insights into the reason why we are attracted to puzzles: "The fact is that our lives are largely spent in solving puzzles; for what is a puzzle but a perplexing question? And from our childhood upwards we are perpetually asking questions or trying to answer them."

CHAPTER 6

Domino Logic Puzzles

You have a row of dominoes set up; you knock over the first one, and what will happen to the last one is that it will go over very quickly.
—DWIGHT D. EISENHOWER (1890–1969)

Dominoes were likely invented in China in the 1100s and introduced into Italy in the 1700s. From there they spread to Europe. Like cards, they have provided opportunities for playing all kinds of games. A regular set has twenty-eight dominoes. A line divides each piece, called a "tile," into two sections. Each section has one to six spots, called "pips," on it. Every possible combination of spots appears in a domino set, and no two dominoes are the same. This chapter has puzzles made by using dominoes, similar in logical thinking (but also different) to the puzzles in Chapter 1. Once again, you will have to put on your thinking cap, because these require a large dose of reasoning. The final five puzzles are based on a combination of cards and dominoes, just for the fun of it.

The Missing Domino

The puzzles in this section are like the missing-card puzzles in Chapter 1. The difference is that you have to identify the missing domino, and this requires a slightly different kind of thinking. Let's go through a simple one together for the sake of illustration.

▶ ILLUSTRATION ◀

The dominoes form a sequence according to a rule. The last one is missing. Which one is it of the options given?

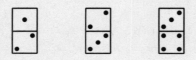

Choose the missing domino:

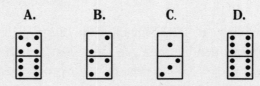

The rule is that the number of spots on both the top and bottom parts of the dominoes increases by one. Look at the top spots and you will see the application of this rule:

one spot—two spots—three spots—four spots

The missing tile must thus have five spots on the top. Now look at the bottom spots in order and you will see a sequence starting with two spots as follows:

two spots—three spots—four spots—five spots

So the bottom part of the missing domino must have six spots. Option A is thus the correct answer.

For the following three puzzles, you are given hints to get you warmed up for the harder puzzles.

Puzzle 1

The following row of dominoes is constructed according to a rule. Of the given options, which domino completes the row? **Hint:** consider the number of spots on top and bottom on each successive domino.

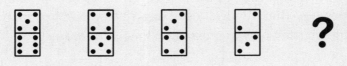

Choose the missing domino:

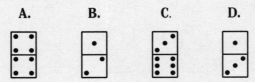

Puzzle 2

Twelve dominoes are placed in each row according to a rule. Of the options given, which one is the missing domino? **Hint:** look at the number of spots on the top and bottom parts of the final tile in each row.

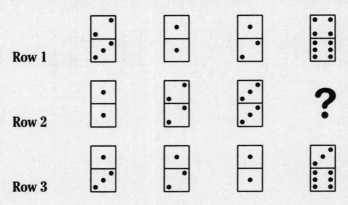

Choose the missing domino:

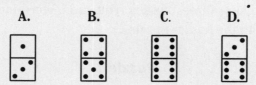

Puzzle 3

Twelve dominoes in another layout are placed in each row according to a different rule. Of the options given, which one is the missing domino? **Hint:** simply look at how the top and bottom parts of the tiles in each row progress, from the first to the last.

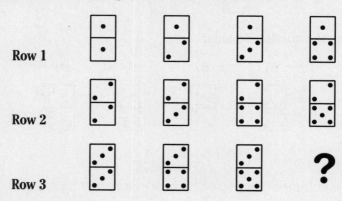

Choose the missing domino:

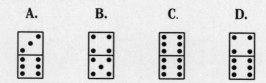

▶ MODERATELY HARD ◀

No more hints are given for the remainder of the puzzles in this section. Good luck!

Puzzle 4

Let's change the pace a bit and work with domino fractions. The top domino is the numerator of the fraction and the bottom one is the denominator. Each fraction is constructed according to a rule. Of the options given, which domino is the denominator of the final fraction?

Fraction 1 **Fraction 2** **Fraction 3** **Fraction 4**

Choose the missing domino:

A. B. C. D.

Puzzle 5

Let's do another fraction puzzle. Each fraction is constructed according to a rule. Of the options given, which domino is the denominator of the final fraction?

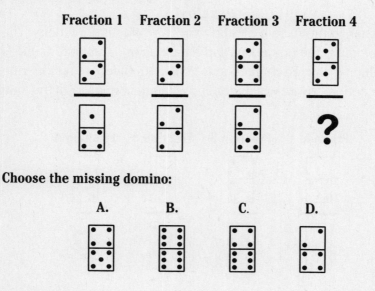

Choose the missing domino:

Dominoes may go back in time considerably. The ancient Babylonians used numbered clay tiles for accounting purposes. These could easily have been used to play games as well and, hence, could possibly be the forerunners of dominoes.

Puzzle 6

Here's one last fraction puzzle. Once again, each fraction is constructed according to a rule. Of the options given, which domino is the denominator of the final fraction?

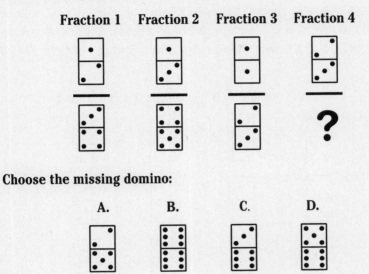

Choose the missing domino:

Puzzle 7

Following is a set of five dominoes. Each domino is included in the set according to a specific rule. One is missing from the set. Of the options given, which domino is that?

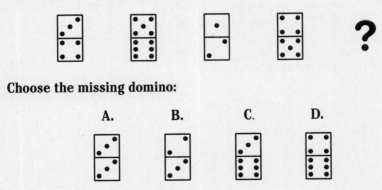

Choose the missing domino:

Are you ready for much more challenging puzzles?

Puzzle 8

Four dominoes are placed in each of four columns. At the bottom of each column you will see a number. There is a pattern here. Can you figure it out? Choose the missing number at the bottom of Column 4.

Column 1	Column 2	Column 3	Column 4

24   **28**   **26**   **?**

Choose the missing number:

A. 28   B. 22   C. 25   D. 27

Puzzle 9

Here is a similar puzzle, but the rule here is different. What is the missing number this time?

Column 1	Column 2	Column 3	Column 4

9   **2**   **3**   **?**

Choose the missing number:

A. 7   B. 5   C. 9   D. 6

Now that you might have a knack for this type of puzzle, let's do one more. The rule is again different. What is the missing number this time?

Column 1	Column 2	Column 3	Column 4

15	**24**	**10**	**?**

Choose the missing number:

A. 23	B. 16	C. 14	D. 19

Dominoes are played all over the world, but they are especially popular throughout the Caribbean islands. Each island has its own traditions and rules for playing the game.

The Odd Domino Out

As in the case of the odd-card-out puzzles in Chapter 1, in this section the challenge is to identify a domino in a set or layout that does not belong there. Let's do one together.

▸ ILLUSTRATION ◂

The dominoes in each column are placed there according to a rule. Which domino does not fit in?

Column 1	Column 2	Column 3	Column 4

In each column a spot is added to the spots on the top and bottom parts of the first or top tile to produce the tile below it. So in the first column the top tile has one spot on its top part and four on its bottom part. The tile below it will have one more spot in each part—two spots on top and five on the bottom.

Look at the top tile in Column 4. It has three spots in its top part and five spots in its bottom part. According to the rule, the bottom tile should have four spots on top and six on the bottom, but it has one on top and six on the bottom. So this is the odd domino out.

For the following three puzzles, you are given hints to get you warmed up for the harder puzzles.

Puzzle 11

The following sequence of six dominoes constitutes a set—that is, each domino has a specific feature that allows it to belong in the set. But one does not. Can you detect it? **Hint:** look at the number of spots on the top and bottom parts of each tile—there is a constant relation between the two numbers in each tile, except one.

Tile 1	Tile 2	Tile 3	Tile 4	Tile 5	Tile 6

Puzzle 12

The following sequence has been constructed in a specific way, with each domino following the other according to a rule. But one does not. Which one is it? **Hint:** just look at how the number of spots on top and bottom progress one tile after the other.

Tile 1	Tile 2	Tile 3	Tile 4	Tile 5	Tile 6

The term "domino effect" comes from the chain reaction that is set off by tipping the first standing domino in a line of standing dominoes, causing the whole line to topple. It is used in political theory to refer to any event in one nation that will cause similar events in neighboring nations.

Puzzle 13

The dominoes in each column are placed there according to a rule. Which column does not fit in?

Column 1	Column 2	Column 3	Column 4

▸ MODERATELY HARD ◂

No more hints are given for the remainder of the puzzles in this section. Good luck!

Puzzle 14

In the following set of dominoes, each tile except one displays a specific numerical pattern. Which one does not follow the pattern?

Tile 1	Tile 2	Tile 3	Tile 4	Tile 5	Tile 6	Tile 7

Puzzle 15

Here's a similar puzzle. Again, in the set of dominoes, each tile except one displays a specific numerical pattern (different from the previous puzzle). Which one does not follow the pattern?

Tile 1	Tile 2	Tile 3	Tile 4	Tile 5	Tile 6	Tile 7

Puzzle 16

Let's get back to a previous type of puzzle, with a bit of a difference, of course. Four dominoes are placed in each of five columns. At the bottom of each column you will see a number. There is a pattern here. Can you figure it out? If so, which column is the odd one out?

Column 1	Column 2	Column 3	Column 4	Column 5

7/13 **13/20** **9/18** **11/20** **12/15**

Puzzle 17

Here's another one to test your domino logic again. Four dominoes are placed in each of five columns. At the bottom of each column you will see a number. There is a pattern here. Can you figure it out? If so, which column is the odd one out?

Column 1	Column 2	Column 3	Column 4	Column 5

11   **11**   **5**   **6**   **11**

Domino toppling has become a game of its own. A competition called Domino Day was established in the Netherlands in 1986. The goal of the competition is to knock over the greatest number of dominoes. In one competition over 4 million dominoes were toppled!

The last three puzzles in this section switch to rows rather than columns. In each row the tiles are numbered consecutively, from Tile 1 to Tile 5.

Puzzle 18

The tiles in each of the five rows are in a sequence according to a rule. One of the rows is the odd one out. Which one is it?

	Tile 1	Tile 2	Tile 3	Tile 4	Tile 5
Row 1					

	Tile 1	Tile 2	Tile 3	Tile 4	Tile 5
Row 2					

	Tile 1	Tile 2	Tile 3	Tile 4	Tile 5
Row 3					

	Tile 1	Tile 2	Tile 3	Tile 4	Tile 5
Row 4					

	Tile 1	Tile 2	Tile 3	Tile 4	Tile 5
Row 5					

Puzzle 19

Let's do another one. Tiles are inserted in each of the five rows in sequence according to a rule. One of the rows is the odd one out. Which one is it?

	Tile 1	Tile 2	Tile 3	Tile 4	Tile 5
Row 1					

	Tile 1	Tile 2	Tile 3	Tile 4	Tile 5
Row 2					

	Tile 1	Tile 2	Tile 3	Tile 4	Tile 5
Row 3					

	Tile 1	Tile 2	Tile 3	Tile 4	Tile 5
Row 4					

	Tile 1	Tile 2	Tile 3	Tile 4	Tile 5
Row 5					

Puzzle 20

In this puzzle, as before, the tiles are inserted in each of the five rows in a sequence according to a rule. One of the rows is the odd one out. Which one is it?

	Tile 1	Tile 2	Tile 3	Tile 4	Tile 5
Row 1					
Row 2					
Row 3					
Row 4					
Row 5					

Dominoes Meet Cards

The five puzzles in this final section involve a combination of cards and dominoes. Anything goes here. They vary in difficulty level. Some are harder than others. Let's do one for the sake of illustration.

▶ ILLUSTRATION ◀

The cards and dominoes have been placed in each row according to a rule. Of the options given, what's the missing card in the bottom row?

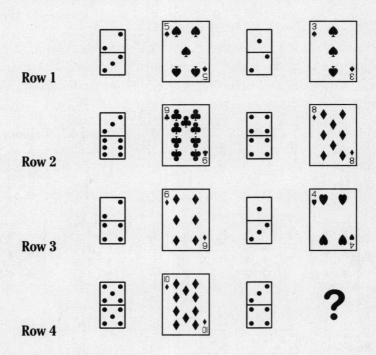

Choose the missing card:

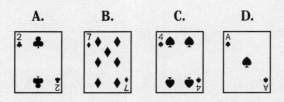

Did you miss the pattern? Add the spots on a domino and you get the number value of the card after it in a row. That's it. Consider Row 1. The spots in the first tile add up to five, and that's the number value of the card. The next domino has three spots in total, and that's the number value of the card after it, ending the row. Missing from the fourth row is a card with a number value seven. The answer is thus B. Note that the suit of the card is irrelevant in this case.

These puzzles are quite complex and may involve spots, number values, suits, and other possibilities. Good luck!

Puzzle 21

Let's start off with a relatively easy one. In each column, the top domino and bottom card are connected logically in some way. One of the columns, however, does not fit the pattern. Which one is that?

| Column 1 | Column 2 | Column 3 | Column 4 | Column 5 |

Puzzle 22

This is a bit harder. The domino and two cards in each column are connected in some specific way. What's the missing domino, of the options given, in the fifth column?

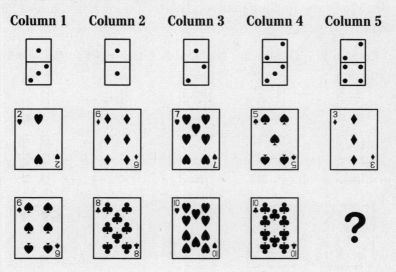

| Column 1 | Column 2 | Column 3 | Column 4 | Column 5 |

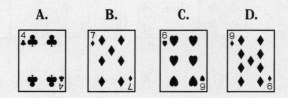

Choose the missing card:

A.   B.   C.   D.

Puzzle 23

This puzzle is harder than the previous two. The two dominoes and two cards in each column are connected in some specific way, indicated by the bottom number. An ace has the numerical value of 1. What's the missing number, of the options given, in the fifth column?

Column 1	Column 2	Column 3	Column 4	Column 5

6	5	5	8	?

Choose the missing number:

A. 8   B. 7   C. 9   D. 3

Puzzle 24

Here's one more. Be careful! There is a bit of a trick here. The three dominoes and the bottom card in each column are connected in some specific way. But one column does not fit in. Which one is that?

Column 1	Column 2	Column 3	Column 4

Puzzle 25

Here's one last puzzle of this kind. The two dominoes and two cards in each column are connected in some specific way. What's the missing number, of the options given, in the fifth column?

Column 1   Column 2   Column 3   Column 4   Column 5

Choose the missing card:

A.   B.   C.   D.

CHAPTER 7

Number Logic Puzzles

*A good decision is based on knowledge
and not on numbers.*
—PLATO (C. 429–347 B.C.E.)

The great ancient philosopher and mathematician Pythagoras believed that numbers were the key to understanding reality. He founded the Pythagorean Brotherhood around 500 B.C.E. to study number patterns, believing firmly that knowledge of the universe would come from contemplating these patterns. It turned out he was right. Numbers do indeed form patterns. Let's become entangled in some of these patterns in the following twenty-five puzzles. You will have to figure out how the numbers relate to each other in some given arrangement or layout.

The Missing Number

In most of the puzzles in this section, you will be given four grids with numbers in them. One of the numbers will be missing. You have to figure out what that number is—there is only one solution! Let's do a simple one together.

▸ ILLUSTRATION ◂

The numbers in each grid are related logically to each other according to the same rule applied to all the four grids. What's the missing number?

2		3
	10	
4		1

4		8
	18	
2		4

12		2
	16	
1		1

9		1
	?	
5		0

The answer is 15. Here's the rule: add the numbers in the four corners of the grid to produce the middle number. In the leftmost grid, the sum of the four corner numbers is 10 ($2 + 3 + 4 + 1 = 10$), and that is the number in the center. This rule applies to all the grids:

Second grid: $4 + 8 + 2 + 4 = 18$

Third grid: $12 + 2 + 1 + 1 = 16$

So the missing number in the last grid is 15 ($9 + 1 + 5 + 0 = 15$).

Note that you are not given options to choose from, as in previous chapters! It's time to put on your number logic cap on!

▸ EASY ◂

For the following three puzzles, you are given hints just to get you warmed up for the harder puzzles.

Puzzle 1

All four number grids are constructed with the same rule. The middle number in the final grid is missing. What is that number? **Hint:** look for two operations—addition and doubling.

1		3
	20	
4		2

2		1
	18	
2		4

3		7
	54	
9		8

9		6
	?	
1		7

Puzzle 2

Here's another puzzle. Again, the following four number grids are constructed with the same rule. The middle number in the final grid is missing. What is that number? **Hint:** look for some operation other than addition as the hidden pattern.

2		3
	36	
2		3

4		5
	120	
1		6

7		7
	147	
3		1

5		6
	?	
3		2

Puzzle 3

As before, the following four number grids are constructed with the same rule. The middle number in the final grid is missing. What is that number? **Hint:** this is a little more complex than the previous ones. Look for two operations applied to the corner numbers in order to produce the middle one.

8		6
	8	
4		2

5		9
	9	
3		2

12		12
	10	
8		6

15		12
	?	
13		6

▶ MODERATELY HARD ◀

No more hints are given for the remainder of the puzzles in this section. Also, this time the arithmetic is harder because all the cells are filled in, and thus you will have to use more complex logic to figure out how the grids are constructed. Good luck!

Puzzle 4

The following four number grids are constructed with the same rule. A number is missing from the final grid. What is that number?

2	4	3
6	7	2
4	2	1

10	1	2
5	3	4
1	0	5

8	1	2
1	11	3
3	2	0

7	?	1
3	3	2
5	2	4

Puzzle 5

Here's another one. The following four number grids are constructed with the same rule. A number is missing from the final grid. What is that number?

1	2	4
8	16	32
64	128	256

4	8	16
32	64	128
256	512	1024

2	4	8
16	32	64
128	256	512

3	6	12
24	48	96
192	384	?

Puzzle 6

The following four number grids are constructed with the same rule. A number is missing from the final grid. What is that number?

4	9	3
10	1	7
4	8	8

10	9	7
7	8	7
1	1	4

5	1	16
12	15	1
1	2	1

12	6	9
2	7	4
4	5	?

Puzzle 7

Let's do one more. The following four number grids are constructed with the same rule. A number is missing from the final grid. What is that number?

20	2	1
10	10	3
9	9	5

11	11	1
7	8	8
19	1	3

12	9	2
5	16	2
6	10	7

9	8	6
12	8	3
5	?	15

▶ DIFFICULT ◀

In the puzzles in this section you are given different grids. The numbers in the grids form a pattern. You have to find the missing number.

Puzzle 8

The numbers in each row form a pattern. What number is missing from the final cell in the fifth row, thus completing the grid logically?

Row 1	8	5	2	4	7
Row 2	10	2	3	3	6
Row 3	11	7	5	4	9
Row 4	15	5	4	3	13
Row 5	12	3	5	1	?

Puzzle 9

The numbers in each column form a pattern. What number is missing from the third column, thus completing the grid logically?

Column 1	Column 2	Column 3	Column 4	Column 5
2	4	8	8	6
4	4	2	3	5
3	5	1	2	1
7	3	?	2	4
63	39	55	26	48

Puzzle 10

Let's do one more. What number belongs in the empty cell, given that the numbers in the grid are inserted according to a pattern? Good luck!

2	5	7	6	3
8	3	1	4	7
5	2	7	5	4
6	5	4	4	4
2	8	4	4	?

The Pythagoreans believed that each natural number stood for something symbolic. For instance, the number 1 stood for unity, reason, and creation. This is why they thought the single horn of the unicorn possessed magical powers. In the form of an amulet, it continues to have this meaning in many cultures, where it is purported to cure diseases and neutralize the poisonous bites of snakes and rabid dogs.

Number-Letter Codes

Replacing numbers with letters and vice versa is an ancient activity, found in all forms of secret writing and, of course, in many branches of mathematics. The basis of making secret codes, in fact, consists in replacing one set of symbols with another according to some code. In this section you will be involved in puzzles, called Number-Letter Codes, that will test your logical skills in this area. Let's do a puzzle together for the sake of illustration.

The term "Pythagorean Brotherhood" is likely a mistranslation, or an older English translation, because Pythagoras encouraged women to participate fully in his so-called "brotherhood." Late in life, he married one of his students, Theano. An accomplished cosmologist and healer, Theano headed the Pythagorean society after her husband's death and, even though she faced persecution, continued to spread the Pythagorean philosophy throughout Egypt and Greece alongside her daughters.

▶ ILLUSTRATION ◀

Each letter from A to E stands for one of the five numbers listed. No two letters have the same numerical value. Match each letter to its number as indicated by the equations, thus unraveling the hidden code.

NUMBER LIST: 1, 4, 5, 6, 9

- $A = C + D$
- $B = A + D$
- $E = C + A$

CODE

A	B	C	D	E

The only substitutions that will make these equations work are as follows:

A	B	C	D	E
5	9	1	4	6

This code produces the given equations:

- $5 = 1 + 4$
- $9 = 5 + 4$
- $6 = 1 + 5$

Trying out any other replacement code will not work, as you might want to find out for yourself. As you can see, both trial and error and number reasoning are involved here.

▸ EASY ◂

As warm-up to the harder puzzles, try these easy ones first.

Puzzle 11

Each letter from A to D stands for one of the four numbers listed. No two letters have the same numerical value. Match each letter to its number as indicated by the equations, thus unraveling the hidden code.

NUMBER LIST: 1, 2, 3, 5
- $A = D + B$
- $B = D + C$
- $D = C + C$

CODE

A	B	C	D

Puzzle 12

Here's another easy one, just to get you going. Each letter from A to E stands for one of the five numbers listed. No two letters have the same numerical value. Match each letter to its number as indicated by the equations, thus unraveling the hidden code.

NUMBER LIST: 1, 2, 3, 4, 5

- $A = B + B$
- $C = A + A$
- $D = A + B$
- $E = A + D$
- $E = C + B$

CODE

A	B	C	D	E

Puzzle 13

One more fairly easy one, but maybe not so easy. Each letter from A to F stands for one of the six numbers listed. No two letters have the same numerical value. Match each letter to its number as indicated by the equations, thus unraveling the hidden code.

NUMBER LIST: 1, 4, 5, 6, 9, 10

- $A = B + C$
- $E = A + C$
- $D = A + B$
- $F = D + C$
- $F = A + C + B$

CODE

A	B	C	D	E	F

▶ MODERATELY HARD ◀

It's time to move on to some harder puzzles.

Puzzle 14

In this puzzle each letter from A to F stands for one of the six numbers listed. No two letters have the same numerical value. Match each letter to its number as indicated by the equations, thus unraveling the hidden code.

NUMBER LIST: 1, 2, 3, 5, 6, 11

- $F = C + D$
- $F = D + D + E$
- $F = C + B + A$
- $C = D + E$

- $C = B + A + E$
- $D = B + A$
- $B = E + A$
- $A = E + E$

CODE

A	B	C	D	E	F

Puzzle 15

Let's make the code a little bigger. This time each letter from A to G stands for one of the seven numbers listed. No two letters have the same numerical value. Match each letter to its number as indicated by the equations, thus unraveling the hidden code.

NUMBER LIST: 1, 3, 4, 5, 6, 7, 10

- $B = A + A$
- $B = A + D + C$
- $G = F + C$
- $B = F + D$
- $B = F + E + C$

- $G = D + E$
- $A = D + C$
- $F = A + C$
- $D = E + C$

CODE

A	B	C	D	E	F	G

Puzzle 16

Here's a more challenging one. Each letter from A to H stands for one of the eight numbers listed. No two letters have the same numerical value. Match each letter to its number as indicated by the equations, thus unraveling the hidden code.

NUMBER LIST: 1, 3, 4, 5, 6, 7, 10, 15

- $E = F + G$
- $F = C + B$
- $F = H + H + B$
- $E = F + B + A$
- $F = D + H$
- $E = D + H + G$
- $F = G + G$
- $E = D + H + B + A$
- $F = G + B + A$

- $D = B + H$
- $D = C + A$
- $D = G + A + A$
- $C = H + H$
- $C = G + A$
- $G = B + A$
- $G = H + A + A$
- $B = H + A$

CODE

A	B	C	D	E	F	G	H

Puzzle 17

To give you a respite from logical complexity, here's a puzzle that is a lot easier, just before it's going to get a lot harder in the last three puzzles. Each letter from A to E stands for one of the five numbers listed. No two letters have the same numerical value. Match each letter to its number as indicated by the equations, thus unraveling the hidden code.

NUMBER LIST: 4, 5, 6, 10, 15

- $A = E + E$
- $A = C + D$
- $B = E + E + E$
- $B = A + E$
- $B = C + D + E$

CODE

A	B	C	D	E

▶ DIFFICULT ◀

Note that several operations may be involved in the equations, including addition, subtraction, and multiplication. Good luck!

Puzzle 18

Each letter from A to F stands for one of the six numbers listed. No two letters have the same numerical value. Match each letter to its number as indicated by the equations, thus unraveling the hidden code. Note that addition and subtraction are involved.

NUMBER LIST: 2, 4, 5, 9, 10, 12

- $A = E + B + B$
- $F = C - B$
- $A = E + D$
- $C = F + B$
- $E = A - D$

- $C = F + B$
- $B = C - F$
- $C = D + D + D$
- $D = B + B$
- $E = F - E$

CODE

A	B	C	D	E	F

Puzzle 19

Each letter from A to G stands for one of the seven numbers listed. No two letters have the same numerical value. Match each letter to its number as indicated by the equations, thus unraveling the hidden code. Note that addition and subtraction are involved.

NUMBER LIST: 1, 4, 5, 7, 9, 10, 11

- $C = A - D$
- $A = D + C$
- $D = F - A$
- $E = B + C$
- $B = E - C$
- $B = G + D - C$
- $D = E - G$

- $C = B - F$
- $C = E - B$
- $A = B - A$
- $A = F - A + C$
- $B = F + C$
- $B = A + A$

CODE

A	B	C	D	E	F	G

The decimal system is also called the Hindu-Arabic system because it was developed by Hindu mathematicians in India more than 2,000 years ago. The Arabs learned to use this system in the 700s, spreading it throughout the Middle East, northern Africa, and Spain. The idea of a position to represent a number value was actually known to many other ancient civilizations, including the Aztecs and Mayans.

Puzzle 20

Each letter from A to F stands for one of the six numbers listed. No two letters have the same numerical value. Match each letter to its number as indicated by the equations, thus unraveling the hidden code. Note that addition, subtraction, and multiplication are involved. Good luck!

NUMBER LIST: 3, 4, 6, 7, 8, 9

- $A = B \times C - A$
- $A = B + C$
- $A = E + D - B$
- $B = F \times C - B$
- $C = F \times C - A$
- $F = D + B - A$

- $A = D + B - F$
- $E = A + D - E$
- $E = D + D - B$
- $D = F + C$
- $D = B + F - C$

CODE

A	B	C	D	E	F

Anything Goes

The five puzzles in this final section also involve number logic skills, as in the previous sections. But anything goes here, as you will see. They vary in difficulty level, though. Some are harder than others. Good luck!

Puzzle 21

The number on each step follows logically from the one below it. What number belongs on the top step—160, 162, 164, or 168?

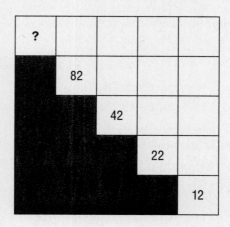

Puzzle 22

What number does the letter A stand for based on the hidden code used to construct each column?

Column 1	Column 2	Column 3	Column 4
2	A	7	16
5	9	15	A
11	12	A	4
A	39	40	38

Puzzle 23

The center number in each triangle is related to the numbers on the three vertices according to a rule of formation. What is the missing number in the last triangle?

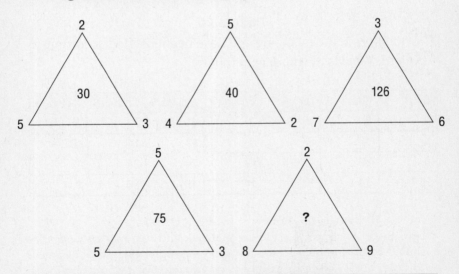

Number symbolism is universal. In America, many try to avoid thirteen because it is felt to be an unlucky number. In parts of Ghana, seven is considered to be an ominous number and is always spoken as "six plus one." In parts of northern Africa, five is considered a protective number, since there are five fingers on the human hand.

Puzzle 24

Each grid (one to the left and one to the right of the black separation) contains numbers placed in relation to each other in a certain way—that is, the numbers in Grid 1 are connected to the numbers in Grid 2 in some logical way. Can you figure out what the missing number is?

Grid 1 **Grid 2**

2	3	5		4	6	10
1	6	9		2	12	18
7	8	10		14	?	20

Puzzle 25

The numbers in the following grid have been inserted according to a pattern. What is the missing number?

Column 1	Column 2	Column 3	Column 4	Column 5	Column 6	Column 7
2	8	1	3	6	7	5
4	16	2	6	12	14	10
8	32	4	12	24	28	20
16	64	8	24	48	56	?

Lord Byron once wrote, "I know that two and two make four and should be glad to prove it too if I could—though I must say if by any sort of process I could convert two and two into five it would give me much greater pleasure."

CHAPTER 8

Lie Detection Puzzles

If you tell the truth, you don't have to remember anything.
—MARK TWAIN (1835–1910)

What is truth? From the dawn of civilization, this question has intrigued great thinkers, artists, writers, scientists, and many others. But it is also a more modest question that puzzlemakers like to pose, as we have seen already in Chapter 5. There exists another popular variety of puzzles that plays artfully on truthful and mendacious statements and what conclusions we can draw from these. It goes by various names, but we will use the term *Lie Detection* here, using a bit of poetic license, of course, because we are not involved in actually detecting lies, which is a forensic science all its own. Puzzles that fall within this genre typically contain statements, a certain number of which are true and others false. In the first two sections of this chapter, your task is to test the logical consistency of these statements in order to identify a culprit. The final section of the chapter contains puzzles that present boxes with misleading labels, and you will have to figure out the real contents of the boxes, despite the labels. Again, you will need to use straightforward logical reasoning.

Who's the Culprit?

The first set of puzzles involves five people who make statements to interrogators, some of which are true and others false. You are told exactly how many true and false statements there are in the set of five. Then, on the basis of these statements, you have to figure out, using logic, who the culprit is among the five. Let's do one together for the sake of illustration.

▶ ILLUSTRATION ◀

Five gangsters were brought in for questioning yesterday. One was known to have murdered a gangster from another gang. Here's what each one said. As it turns out, three of the statements were true and two were false. Can you identify the killer on the basis of their statements?

Dick:	I didn't do it.
Don:	Dick is innocent.
Dirk:	Dick didn't do it.
Dale:	Dick did it.
Devin:	I am innocent.

Let's start with the first three statements. All three indicate the same thing, in different ways, of course—namely, that Dick is innocent. Dick declares his innocence outright, and the other two, Don and Dirk, agree. So these three statements are either all true or all false. We are told that there were three true statements and two false ones in the set. They cannot be all false because there were only two—not three—false ones. So we can safely deduce that they were all true.

This means that the remaining two statements, by Dale and Devin, were the false ones. Let's see what each one said. Dale said that Dick is the culprit. Well, this is false, as we just deduced. It changes nothing, so far. But look at Devin's statement. He says that he is innocent. This statement, as we now know, is one of the two false ones. Contrary to what he says, Devin is our killer.

▶ EASY ◀

Just to get started, try these very simple puzzles.

Puzzle 1

Five people were interrogated yesterday. One was known to have murdered an acquaintance because of rage. Here's what each one said. All the statements were true. Can you identify the killer?

Andy:	*I didn't do it.*
Art:	*I didn't do it, either.*
Alexa:	*I didn't do it.*
Ariana:	*I am innocent.*
Alina:	*Alexa is innocent.*

Puzzle 2

Five individuals were questioned yesterday. One was suspected of having robbed a bank. Here's what each one said. All the statements were false. Can you identify the robber?

Bob:	*Ben did it.*
Brent:	*No, Barb did it.*
Bertha:	*No, Bob did it.*
Barb:	*I don't know who did it.*
Ben:	*Bertha did it.*

Puzzle 3

Five workers from the same company were brought in for questioning yesterday. One was suspected of having embezzled company funds. Here's what each one said. Four statements were true and one was false. The false one was uttered by the embezzler. Can you identify the embezzler?

Cam: I didn't do it.
Charlotte: Cam is innocent.
Carroll: I didn't do it.
Claudia: Carroll is innocent.
Chuck: I didn't do it.

▸ MODERATELY HARD ◂

It's time to try your hand at harder puzzles.

Puzzle 4

Five gangsters were questioned by the police yesterday. One was suspected of having murdered a rival in another gang. Here's what each one said. Two statements were true and the other three were false. Strangely, the killer was one of the two who told the truth! Can you identify the killer?

Evan: Elvira did it.
Eric: Evan lied.
Elana: Elvira's the killer.
Emma: Yeah, Elvira is the killer.
Elvira: Evan lied.

Puzzle 5

Five people were interrogated yesterday. One was suspected of having stolen money from a bank machine. Here's what each one said. Three statements were true and the other two were false. Can you identify the thief?

Frank:	Felicia is the robber.
Fanny:	Faustus is the robber.
Filomena:	Frank is the robber.
Faustus:	I am innocent.
Felicia:	I am innocent.

Puzzle 6

Five friends were interrogated yesterday. One was suspected of having murdered a paramour. Here's what each one said. Two statements were true and the other three were false. Can you identify the killer?

Grant:	I didn't do it.
Glenda:	I didn't do it.
Gabby:	I didn't do it.
Gaston:	Glenda did it.
Gail:	Grant did it.

Puzzle 7

Five colleagues were brought in for questioning yesterday. One was suspected of having murdered a coworker out of jealousy. Here's what each one said. Two statements were true and the other three were false. Can you identify the killer?

Hank:	I didn't do it.
Helen:	Hank is innocent.
Harry:	I didn't do it.
Hanna:	I didn't do it.
Hubert:	Hank is innocent.

Lies often go undetected because we do not attempt to detect them. This phenomenon is called the ostrich effect by psychologists.

Are you ready for more challenging puzzles? Have fun!

Puzzle 8

Five coworkers were interrogated yesterday. One was suspected of having stolen company funds. Here's what each one said. Two statements were true and three were false. Can you identify the thief?

Inez:	*I didn't do it.*
Irene:	*Inez didn't do it.*
Ida:	*Ivan didn't do it.*
Iris:	*Inez did it.*
Ivan:	*Inez did it.*

Puzzle 9

Five renowned hackers were questioned yesterday. One was suspected of having hacked a top-secret government site. Here's what each one said. Three statements were true and two were false. Strangely, the hacker was one of the truth tellers. Can you identify the hacker?

Jack:	*Jane is innocent.*
Jane:	*I am innocent.*
Jim:	*Jane did it.*
Jenna:	*Jack is innocent.*
Jill:	*Jane is innocent.*

In 1730, the British novelist Daniel Defoe wrote an essay in which he recommended taking the pulse of a suspected criminal in order to determine if he or she was lying.

Puzzle 10

Five people were interrogated yesterday. One was suspected of having murdered a romantic rival. Here's what each one said. Two statements were true and the other three were false. Can you identify the killer?

Kyle: *I'm innocent.*

Karen: *I'm innocent.*

Ken: *Karen is the killer.*

Kristina: *Kayla is innocent.*

Kayla: *Kyle is the killer.*

Who's the Culprit This Time?

In this next set of puzzles, each person makes two statements, and you are told again how many statements are true or false. This variant adds more complexity to the kind of logic that is required. Enjoy!

▶ ILLUSTRATION ◀

Five people who all knew each other were interrogated yesterday. One was suspected of having murdered a secret romantic rival. Each one made two statements. Here are all the statements. There were eight true statements in total and two false ones. Can you identify the killer?

Sam: *(1) Simon is innocent.*
(2) Shirley didn't do it.

Sarah: *(3) Shirley is innocent.*
(4) Simon is innocent.

Simon: *(5) I am innocent.*
(6) Sarah told the truth.

Shirley: *(7) Simon did it.*
(8) Sam didn't do it.

Sally: *(9) Shirley didn't do it.*
(10) Simon is innocent.

Statements (2), (3), and (9) indicate the same thing—namely, that Shirley is innocent. These statements are thus all true or all false. They cannot be false because there were only two, not three, false statements in the set. Similar reasoning can be applied to statements (1), (5), and (10), which indicate the same thing—namely, that Simon is innocent. The three statements cannot be all false, since as we know there were only two false statements in the set. So they are true. And this means that Shirley and Simon are indeed innocent.

This makes six true statements so far. There were eight in total, so there were two other true statements in the set. Look at Sarah's statement (4). She says that Simon is innocent. As we just deduced, this is true. Next, look at Simon's statement (6). He says that Sarah told the truth, and she did by saying that both Shirley and Simon were innocent (as we deduced). We now have identified all eight true statements. This means that statements (7) and (8), both uttered by Shirley, are the two false ones. Her statement (7), "Simon did it," is clearly false. We know he is innocent. But her second statement (8), "Sam didn't do it," is also false. So, contrary to what she says, Sam is our culprit.

▶ EASY ◀

Let's get started with three very easy puzzles.

Puzzle 11

Five gangsters were interrogated yesterday. One was suspected of having murdered a rival gangster. Each one made two statements. Here are the statements, which were all true by the way. Can you identify the killer?

Laura:	(1) I'm innocent.
	(2) Lisa is innocent.
Lenny:	(3) I'm innocent.
	(4) Linda is innocent.

Louise:	(5) Laura told the truth.
	(6) So did Linda.
Linda:	(7) I'm innocent.
	(8) Lenny is innocent.
Lisa:	(9) I'm innocent.
	(10) Laura is innocent.

Puzzle 12

Five hackers were interrogated yesterday. One was suspected of having hacked a company's site. Each one made two statements. Here are the statements, which were all false by the way. Can you identify the hacker?

Mark:	(1) Manny did it.
	(2) I never lie.
Mina:	(3) Melvin did it.
	(4) I never lie.
Melvin:	(5) I never lie.
	(6) Mark did it.
Melissa:	(7) Mina did it.
	(8) I never lie.
Manny:	(9) I never lie.
	(10) Mark did it.

Puzzle 13

Five people were brought in for questioning yesterday. One was suspected of having stolen money from a bank machine. Each one made two statements. Here are their statements. There were nine true statements and one false one. Can you identify the thief?

Nick:	(1) I didn't do it.
	(2) Nando didn't do it.
Nina:	(3) Nathan didn't do it.
	(4) I didn't do it.

Nora:	*(5) I didn't do it.*
	(6) Nick didn't do it.
Nathan:	*(7) I am innocent.*
	(8) Nina didn't do it.
Nando:	*(9) Nick is innocent.*
	(10) I didn't do it.

▸ MODERATELY HARD ◂

The next four puzzles are somewhat harder. Don't get discouraged. Just try them.

Puzzle 14

Five friends were interrogated yesterday. One was suspected of having murdered a paramour. Each one made two statements. Here are all the statements. There were seven true statements and three false ones. Can you identify the murderer?

Paul:	*(1) Pina didn't do it.*
	(2) Pat lied when he said that Pina did it. Don't believe him.
Pina:	*(3) I didn't do it.*
	(4) Pat lied when he said that I did it.
Pete:	*(5) Pina didn't do it.*
	(6) Pat didn't do it.
Pat:	*(7) Pina did it.*
	(8) I didn't do it.
Parth:	*(9) Pat lied when he said that Pina did it.*
	(10) Pina is innocent.

Puzzle 15

Five coworkers were interrogated yesterday. One was suspected of having stolen company funds. Each one made two statements. Here are their statements. There were seven true statements and three false ones. Can you identify the thief?

Ray:	(1) I didn't do it.
	(2) Randy did it.
Rita:	(3) Ray did it.
	(4) I didn't do it.
Raj:	(5) I am innocent.
	(6) Rick is innocent.
Rick:	(7) I am innocent.
	(8) Rita did it.
Randy:	(9) I didn't do it.
	(10) Rita did it.

As long as lies seem to fit into a logical argument, then they will likely be believed. In fact, if your argument isn't logical, it is unlikely to be believed, even if it is true!

Puzzle 16

Five individuals were interrogated yesterday. One was suspected of having robbed a local bank. Each one made two statements. Here are their statements. There were five true statements and five false ones. Interestingly, each individual made exactly one true and one false statement. Can you identify the robber?

Shane:	(1) I didn't do it.
	(2) Steve did it.
Sheila:	(3) I didn't do it.
	(4) Samuel did it.
Samuel:	(5) There were five true statements.
	(6) Shane did it.
Steve:	(7) There were five false statements.
	(8) Sheila did it.
Sandra:	(9) Sheila is innocent.
	(10) I didn't do it.

Puzzle 17

Five gangsters were interrogated yesterday. One was suspected of having killed another gangster. Each one made two statements. Here are their statements. There were eight true statements and two false ones. Can you identify the killer?

Tom:	(1) Tanya didn't do it.
	(2) Tilly didn't do it.
Tina:	(3) Tanya didn't do it.
	(4) Tricia is innocent.
Tricia:	(5) Tanya did it.
	(6) Tom is innocent.
Tilly:	(7) Tanya did it.
	(8) I didn't do it.
Tanya:	(9) Tom didn't do it.
	(10) I didn't do it.

▸ DIFFICULT ◂

Are you ready for more challenging puzzles? Here are three for you!

Puzzle 18

Five people were brought in for questioning yesterday. One was suspected of having murdered a romantic rival. Each one made two statements. Here are their statements. There were five true and five false statements. Can you identify the killer?

Vick:	(1) Vinny did it.
	(2) There were five true statements made to interrogators.
Vera:	(3) Vanna did it.
	(4) I didn't do it.
Valerie:	(5) Vera did it.
	(6) I didn't do it.

Vanna:	(7) I didn't do it.
	(8) Vick is the killer.
Vinny:	(9) I didn't do it.
	(10) There were five false statements made to interrogators.

Puzzle 19

Five hackers were interrogated yesterday. One was suspected of having hacked a military site. Each one made two statements. Here are their statements. There were nine true statements and one false one, made by the hacker. Can you identify the hacker?

Wally:	(1) I didn't do it.
	(2) Will is innocent.
Wendy:	(3) I didn't do it.
	(4) Winny told the truth.
Will:	(5) I didn't do it.
	(6) Winny told the truth.
Wade:	(7) I didn't do it.
	(8) Wendy isn't the hacker.
Winny:	(9) Wally isn't the hacker.
	(10) Will isn't the hacker either.

Puzzle 20

Five people were interrogated yesterday. One was suspected of having been a cold-case serial killer. Each one made two statements. Here are their statements. There were six true statements and four false ones. Can you identify the serial killer?

Zack:	(1) I am not the killer.
	(2) Zilla is innocent.
Zoey:	(3) I am not the killer.
	(4) Zora is the killer.

Zora:	(5) I am not the killer.
	(6) Zubin is the killer.
Zubin:	(7) I am not the killer.
	(8) Zoey is the killer.
Zilla:	(9) Zoey is the killer.
	(10) Zack did it.

Here's an interesting quote about lying from the pen of the great humorist Mark Twain: "One of the most striking differences between a cat and a lie is that a cat has only nine lives."

Misleading Labels

The five puzzles in this final section will challenge your logic skills. You are given three boxes with labels on them. But the labels are all misleading. On that basis you will have to figure out what the real contents of the boxes are. These puzzles vary in difficulty level. Some are harder than others. Let's do one for the purpose of illustration.

▸ ILLUSTRATION ◂

There are three closed boxes on a table that contain, separately, $10, $100, and $1,000. However, they are labeled incorrectly. Someone with a blindfold opens and delves into Box A, pulling out a handful of hundred-dollar bills—five in total. On that basis, can you identify the real contents of each box and label them all correctly?

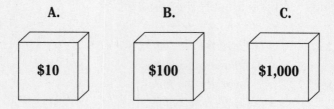

A.	B.	C.
$10	$100	$1,000

There are obviously more than $100 in Box A, since the person took out $500 from it. And, of course, it does not have the $10, as its label erroneously says. So Box A has the $1,000. Now we know that the other two boxes were labeled incorrectly as well. So, what's in Box B? Not the $100 it claims to have, nor the $1,000 that is in Box A. So it contains the $10. This means that Box C is the one with the $100.

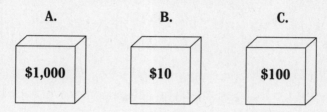

Puzzle 21

There are three closed boxes on a table. One box has two black billiard balls in it, another has two white billiard balls in it, and a third one has one white and one black billiard ball in it. The boxes are labeled, logically enough, BB (two black balls), WW (two white balls), and BW (one black and one white ball). However, the labels have been switched mischievously so that now each box is labeled incorrectly as shown.

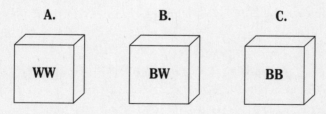

With a blindfold on, someone opens and takes out a white ball from Box B (BW). On that basis, can you identify the real contents of each box and label them correctly?

Puzzle 22

There are three closed boxes on a table that contain, separately, $1, $5, and $20 all in dollar bills. However, they are labeled incorrectly.

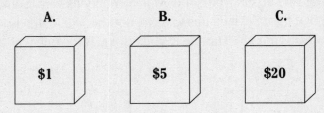

A. $1 **B.** $5 **C.** $20

With a blindfold on, someone opens Box B ($5) and takes eight dollars out. On that basis, can you tell the contents of each box and label them correctly?

Puzzle 23

There are three closed boxes on a table. This time one box has four black billiard balls in it, another has four white billiard balls in it, and a third one has two white and two black billiard balls in it. The boxes are labeled BBBB (four black balls), WWWW (four white balls), and BBWW (two black and two white balls). However, the labels have been switched so that now each box is labeled incorrectly as shown.

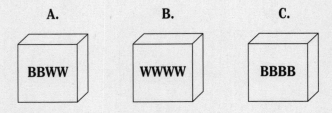

A. BBWW **B.** WWWW **C.** BBBB

With a blindfold on, someone opens and takes out a white ball from Box B (WWWW). On that basis, can you identify the real contents of each box and label them correctly?

Puzzle 24

Let's do another one of these. There are three closed boxes on a table. This time one box has two billiard balls in it, a black and a white one (BW); another has four billiard balls in it, three black and one white (BBBW); and a third one has just one white billiard ball in it (W). The labels have been switched so that now each box is labeled incorrectly as shown.

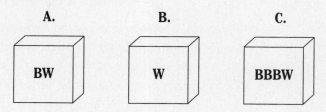

With a blindfold on, someone opens and takes out a black ball from Box A (BW). On that basis, can you identify the real contents of each box and label them correctly?

Puzzle 25

Let's do one last one in this category. There are three closed boxes on a table. This time one box has a single black ball in it (B), another has one white (W), and a third one has a white and black one (BW). The labels have been switched so that now each box is labeled incorrectly as shown.

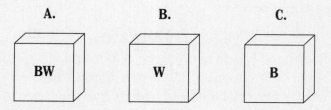

With a blindfold on, someone opens and takes out a black ball from Box C (B). On that basis, can you identify the real contents of each box and label them correctly?

Answers

As a final thought about puzzles, in the hope that you have enjoyed going through the puzzles in this book, let's quote the great Socrates again, who said, "The world's a puzzle; no need to make sense of it."

Chapter 1

Puzzle 1: C

The last three cards in Row B are the same cards as the first three in Row A, but in reverse order. This suggests that the rows are in reverse order. So the missing fourth card in Row A is the first one in Row B—the eight of spades. Just for the sake of completeness, note that in Row A each card is twice the one to its left; in Row B, which is the reverse of Row A, each card is half the one to its left (of course). Also, all four suits are used.

Puzzle 2: D

Each hand has an ace, a three, a four, and a five—but of different suits (of course). Missing from Hand 3 is the four of diamonds. Note that the four of hearts is already used in Hand 1.

Puzzle 3: D

Each hand has the four suits—a heart, a club, a spade, and a diamond. The value of the cards is not relevant. Missing from the fourth hand is a spade, since it has the other three suits.

Puzzle 4: A

There are two parts to the solution. (1) Only the black symbols (spades and clubs) are found in the odd-numbered columns (columns 1, 3, 5), and only the red symbols (hearts and diamonds) are found in the even-numbered columns (columns 2, 4, 6). (2) In each column, the two symbols are alternated; that is, a spade is immediately above or below a club, and a heart is immediately above or below a diamond. So according to this two-part placement system, a heart is missing from the second cell of the second column.

Puzzle 5: C

For each hand, add the number values of the top two cards and you will get the third card down from the top. The fourth or bottom card is a distractor—that is, it is irrelevant to the solution.

Puzzle 6: B

For each hand, the number values of the top two cards and the number values of the bottom two cards, when added together, produce the same total. For the sake of clarity, here are the totals produced by adding the cards in each column according to this pattern: Hand 1: total of 5 (3 + 2 = 4 + 1); Hand 2: total of 8 (5 + 3 = 2 + 6); Hand 3: total of 6 (4 + 2 = 1 + 5); Hand 4: total of 10 (1 + 9 = 8 + 2).

If you look at the grid horizontally instead of vertically, you'll see that D could also work as an answer. How? The numerical value of each row decreases by one. Here are the totals: Row 1: total of 17 (7 + 5 + 4 + 1); Row 2: total of 16 (2 + 3 + 2 + 9); Row 3: total of 15 (4 + 2 + 1 + 8); Row 4: total of 14 (1 + 6 + 5 + 2).

Puzzle 7: A

For this puzzle, you will have to look in both directions—vertically (columns) and horizontally (rows). First, each column has cards of the same suit (all spades, all hearts, all clubs, all diamonds). Second, in each row the number value of the last card to the right is the sum of the values of the previous three cards.

Puzzle 8: C (for Hand 1) and D (for Hand 4)

The sum of the number values of the cards in each column is constant: it is always 15. That is, if you add the value of the cards in the first column you will get 15, as you will in the second, third, and fourth columns.

Puzzle 9: B

Adding the values of the first four cards in a row produces the value of the last card: Row A: $1 + 2 + 4 + 3 = 10$; Row B: $5 + 4 + 2 + 1 = 12$; Row C: $2 + 1 + 2 + 7 = 12$.

Puzzle 10: D

This is a trick puzzle. It is actually easy but is included in the section of difficult puzzles because of the trick itself. Simply note that the final card in a row becomes the first card in the row below it. That's it! There is no other pattern. This is possible because the cards are drawn from the same deck, which is shuffled on different days. Did you look for something more complex just because we put it in the difficult section? You must always be aware with puzzles—a trick may be waiting for you.

Puzzle 11: Column 4

In Column 4, the bottom two cards are in increasing, not decreasing, order: the three of clubs should have been placed before the two of hearts.

Puzzle 12

The five of diamonds in Column 3 should be placed above the seven of hearts and the eight of clubs, since it is lower in value.

Puzzle 13

There is a continuous increasing numerical order to the layout of the cards, starting with a card with the value of 2 in the first column and end- or

ing with a card that should have the numerical value of 13 (the king) in the last spot of the third column. However, there is a queen (numerical value of 12) in that spot with the king above it. So the two are out of order.

Puzzle 14

Here's the "magical order": each card is the sum of the previous two, starting with the third card, of course:

    Card 1
    Card 2
    Card 3 = Card 1 + 2
    Card 4 = Card 2 + 3
    Card 5 = Card 3 + 4

The ace in Row B clearly does not follow this pattern; the card in that spot should be a five, the sum of the first two cards (2 + 3).

Puzzle 15

If it weren't for the king, the cards could be put in numerical sequence as follows: 8–9–10–11–12. But there is a king (value of 13) rather than a queen (value of 12) among the cards. So the king is the card that blocks the sequence.

Puzzle 16: Column 3

Adding the number values of the cards in four of the five columns yields 20. Column 3 does not fit this pattern. Adding the values in that column produces 24.

Puzzle 17: Column 1

In all columns, except the first one, the values of the first four cards when added together produce the value of the card in the bottom cell. For example, in Column 2 the values of the first four cards when added together equal 13 ($6 + 2 + 2 + 3 = 13$), which is the value of the card in the bottom cell, the king. In Column 1, however, the first four cards add up to 22 ($6 + 4 + 6 + 6 = 22$). But there is a king in the bottom cell, which has the value of 13. So the whole column is the culprit column because there is no card that can be put in the bottom cell with the value of 22.

Puzzle 18: Row 4

In the first three rows, add the values of the first three cards; from the resulting sum subtract the value of the fourth. The final result is the value of the last card in the row.

So, for example, in Row 1:
Values of the first three cards added together: $3 + 5 + 2 = 10$
Subtract the value of the fourth card from this: $10 - 3 = 7$
Seven is thus the value of the last card.
This pattern is not applied to Row 4.

Puzzle 19

This puzzle only appears difficult if you miss seeing the simple pattern with which the cards were laid out. The cards are arranged in decreasing order across the rows, starting with a queen ($=12$) in the top left, followed by a jack ($=11$), and so on through the grid until you reach the bottom right corner, where an ace should be. But by mistake there is a four there.

Puzzle 20

This is a tricky puzzle—seemingly difficult, but actually not. The cards in alternate rows have either an even number value or an odd number value.

Row 1: The cards are all odd numbered.

Row 2: The cards are all even numbered.

Row 3: The cards are all odd numbered.

Row 4: The cards are all even numbered except the last one, which is odd numbered.

Puzzle 21

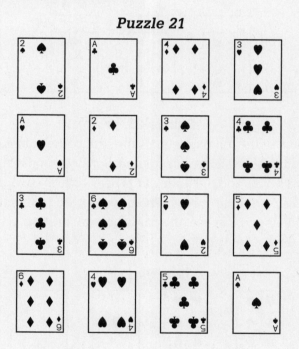

Puzzle 22

If you add the number values in each row, each column, and the two diagonals of the layout, you will get the constant sum of 15.

Puzzle 23: A

The value of the top card equals the sum of the values of the three cards below it in each column. So, for example, the first card is a seven, and the three cards below it are a two, an ace, and a four. So, 7 = 2 + 1 + 4. The missing card is, therefore, a six. And, as you can see, the cards below it are two aces and a four: 6 = 1 + 1 + 4.

Puzzle 24

Here's what the grid looks like with just the number values:

First column: 8 + 3 + 2 = 13 (bottom cell)
Second column: 4 + 5 + 3 = 12 (bottom cell)
Third column: 1 + 7 + 2 = 10 (bottom cell)
Fourth column: 1 + 6 + 6 = 13 (bottom cell)

Puzzle 25

This is really a straightforward observation puzzle. If you look carefully you will see that the five of clubs is repeated twice, and this is impossible, as you know, since there is only one five of clubs in the deck.

Chapter 2

Note: there may be other ways to solve the puzzles in the same number of steps. If so, compare your answers with the ones here.

Puzzle 1

LIFE
wife
wire
wore
WORK

Puzzle 2

WHY
shy
she
sue
SUN

Puzzle 3

SPY
soy
son
sin
WIN

Puzzle 4

FACE
pace
pane
pine
PINK

Puzzle 5

GRADE
graze
craze
CRAZY

Puzzle 6

BLEND
bland
brand (or gland)
grand
GRIND

Puzzle 7

WHILE
whale
shale
stale
STARE

Puzzle 8

BLACK
clack
crack
crank
crane
CRAZE

Puzzle 9

LEAVE
lease
least
beast
boast
TOAST

Puzzle 10

GRAPE
gripe
tripe
trine
twine
swine
SPINE

Puzzle 11

VEIL
live (anagram step)
lice (or dive)
dice
DIME

Puzzle 12

READ
rear (or dear) (anagram step)
hear
heir
HAIR

Puzzle 13

PORE
rope (anagram step)
ripe
rips
LIPS

There could be other answers, but all should involve just three links.

Puzzle 14

EVIL
live (anagram step)
line
mine
mane
NAME (anagram step)

Puzzle 15

TRAP
crap
chap
chop
SHOP

Puzzle 16

LATE
date
dare
read (anagram step)
REAP

Puzzle 17

CHEAP
peach (anagram step)
peace
place
plane
PANEL (anagram step)

Puzzle 18

TRIAL
trail (anagram step)
train (or grail)
grain
groin
grown
FROWN

Puzzle 19

MANE
mare
ream (anagram step)
read
LEAD

Puzzle 20

BASS
base
case
care
race (anagram step)
RATE

Puzzle 21

BRIDE
pride
pried (anagram step)
fried
FREED

Puzzle 22

GRACE
trace
cater (anagram step)
later
laser
loser
LONER

Puzzle 23

BLAME
amble (anagram step)
ample
APPLE

Puzzle 24

LEAD
deal (anagram step)
dial
laid (anagram step)
lair
RAIL (anagram step)

Puzzle 25

TRAP
crap
clap
clip
SLIP

Chapter 3

Puzzle 1

S	E	A
E	N	D
A	D	D

Puzzle 2

R	A	T
A	R	E
T	E	A

Puzzle 3

N	E	W
E	R	A
W	A	S

Puzzle 4

F	A	N
A	C	E
N	E	T

Puzzle 5

G	O	T
O	R	E
T	E	N

Puzzle 6

L	E	A
E	G	G
A	G	E

Puzzle 7

P	A	L
A	L	E
L	E	T

Puzzle 8

S	T	Y
T	W	O
Y	O	U

Puzzle 9

H	U	E
U	S	E
E	E	L

Puzzle 10

C	A	D
A	T	E
D	E	N

Puzzle 11

B	A	B	Y
A	R	E	A
B	E	A	R
Y	A	R	D

Puzzle 12

P	L	O	P
L	O	V	E
O	V	A	L
P	E	L	T

Puzzle 16

G	R	I	N
R	A	R	E
I	R	I	S
N	E	S	T

Puzzle 13

C	L	A	N
L	U	R	E
A	R	E	A
N	E	A	R

Puzzle 17

I	N	T	O
N	E	O	N
T	O	F	U
O	N	U	S

Puzzle 14

A	L	S	O
L	O	O	M
S	O	M	E
O	M	E	N

Puzzle 18

V	I	S	E
I	O	T	A
S	T	I	R
E	A	R	S

Puzzle 15

T	R	O	T
R	O	P	E
O	P	E	N
T	E	N	T

Puzzle 19

D	A	D	A
A	M	E	N
D	E	K	E
A	N	E	W

Puzzle 20

F	L	O	W
L	O	R	E
O	R	B	S
W	E	S	T

Puzzle 21

C	H	E	A	P
H	E	L	L	O
E	L	B	O	W
A	L	O	N	E
P	O	W	E	R

Puzzle 22

R	A	D	A	R
A	L	O	H	A
D	O	Z	E	N
A	H	E	A	D
R	A	N	D	Y

Puzzle 23

L	O	V	E	D
O	P	E	R	A
V	E	N	A	L
E	R	A	S	E
D	A	L	E	S

Puzzle 24

P	L	A	T	E
L	O	V	E	S
A	V	E	R	S
T	E	R	S	E
E	S	S	E	S

Puzzle 25

C	R	A	S	S
R	A	N	C	H
A	N	G	E	R
S	C	E	N	E
S	H	R	E	D

Chapter 4

Puzzle 1: C

All the words refer to items that are typically found in a kitchen. Option C ("platter") is the only one that fits in semantically.

Puzzle 2: A

All the words end with a vowel (a, e, i, o, u). Only option A ("agenda") ends with such a letter.

Puzzle 3: B

The words are all kinship terms. Only option B ("niece") fits semantically into this category.

Puzzle 4: D

The words are laid out in alphabetical order (A–Y), from left to right, starting with "altar" in the top left corner and ending with "yes" in the bottom right corner. Missing from the layout is a word beginning with the letter "l." Option D ("lantern") provides that word.

Puzzle 5: A

The rule is that the number of letters of the words in each column increases by one as you go down the column. So, for example, in Column 1:

at = two letters
the = three letters
full = four letters
enter = five letters
simple = six letters

Missing from Column 5 is a six-letter word, which is provided by option A ("secure").

Puzzle 6: C

The bottom cell in each column is the category to which the four words above belong. For example, in Column 1, the first four words are all "vehicles"—as the last word in the column indicates. The first four words in Column 2 are "buildings," as indicated by option C. For the sake of completeness, the items in Column 3 are "birds," those in Column 4 are "rooms," and those in Column 5 are "sports."

Puzzle 7: B

The sequence starts at the top left and moves horizontally forward (from left to right). The rule is that the last letter of a word becomes the first letter of the next word. So the next word after "tank" must start with "k." Of the options given, only B ("knight") starts with this letter.

Puzzle 8: A

The words in each column are anagrams of each other. So the anagrams of "meal," the top word in Column 3, are "male" and "lame." Option A contains "male."

Puzzle 9: C

Starting at the top of each column, a letter is added to the word in each successively lower cell to produce a new word. For example, in Column 1:

art
arts (adding "s")
marts (adding "m")
smarts (adding "s")

So in Column 3, the missing word is made up of a letter added to the word above it, "hum." Only the word in option C ("chum") is consistent with this rule.

Puzzle 10: D

Each column is a word ladder—do you remember the doublet puzzles in Chapter 2? Let's go through Column 1 for the sake of illustration.

PART (initial word)
pant (changed "r" to "n")
pane (changed "t" to "e")
lane (changed "p" to "l")
LINE (changed "a" to "i")

In Column 2, the final step in the ladder is found in option D. The word ladder is as follows:

TALL
tell
teal
meal
MEAT

Puzzle 11: shore

All the words except "shore" refer to bodies of water or water systems.

Puzzle 12: mean

All the words except "mean" are spelled with double vowel letters—"moon" (two o's), "week" (two e's), and so on.

Puzzle 13: doodle

All the words except "doodle" are spelled with double consonant letters—"better" (two t's), "winner" (two n's), and so on. "Doodle" is spelled with double vowels, not consonants.

Puzzle 14: neck

Each column contains words that belong to the same group or category. Column 1 has color words, Column 2 has geometry words, Column 3 has words referring to musical styles or genres, Column 4 has words referring to parts of the body, and Column 5 has words referring to items of clothing. In that column, however, the word "neck" does not fit in, since it is not an item of clothing.

Puzzle 15: media

Each column has words that end with the same two letters. In Column 1, the words end in "ue"; in Column 2, the words end in "st"; in Column 3, the words end in "ma," except for "media," which ends in "ia"; in Column 4, the words end in "lt"; and in Column 5, the words end in "nd."

Puzzle 16: Column 5: trip-pert

Did you miss this one? It is actually easier than you may have anticipated. Every once in a while we throw in a twist like this. The pairs consist of words that when read backward are also words. So "tips" written backward is "spit." The only pair that breaks this pattern is in Column 5.

Puzzle 17: Column 5: wise

Here's yet another puzzle based on the doublet principle (Chapter 2). Starting at the top, each column is a word ladder. The exception is in Column 5, where the word in the bottom cell should be "wife" not "wise," given that the step above it has the word "life." Changing the letter "l" to "w" makes it "wife" (not "wise").

Puzzle 18: Row 5

In each row, the middle word can be linked to the word before it and the word after it so that two legitimate new words are produced. The exception is Row 5, in which the words cannot be so linked.

Puzzle 19: heck

The words in each column are constructed with the letters of the top word in the column. One example will suffice. In Column 1 the letters of the top word, "rough," are used to make the four words below it:

"rough" = letters: r, o, u, g, h
Choosing r + u + g (from "rough") = "rug"
Choosing h + u + g (from "rough") = "hug"
Choosing o + u + r (from "rough") = "our"
Choosing h + o + g (from "rough") = "hog"

In Column 4, two of the letters—"ck"—in the word "heck" do not belong in the column since they are not found in the top word "shell."

Puzzle 20: glut

Here's a puzzle that is a bit of trick, since the answer is really straightforward. In each column, the word in the bottom cell indicates the theme or category to which the words above it belong. So in Column 1, the first four words are "hockey" terms; in Column 2, the first four words are "mathematics" terms; in Column 3, the first four words refer to "fashion," except for "glut" (the odd word out); in Column 4, the first four words refer to some aspect of "matter"; and in Column 5, the first four words refer to different "media."

Puzzle 21

see	puck	nib
now	smart	pep
pill	new	suck

Puzzle 22: A

The words in a row are spelled with the same vowel. Those in Row 1 have the vowel "a," those in Row 2 have the vowel "e," those in Row 3 have the vowel "i," those in Row 4 have the vowel "o," and those in Row 5 have the vowel "u." Of the given options, only option A ("run") has the required vowel "u."

Puzzle 23: B

The words in each row are spelled with two identical consonants, in various positions within the words. Other consonants can occur in the words. Those in Row 1 are spelled with two b's, those in Row 2 are spelled with two l's, those in Row 3 are spelled with two f's, those in Row 4 are spelled with two s's, and those in Row 5 are spelled with two m's. Of the given options, only option B ("simmer") is spelled with the two m's required by Row 5.

Puzzle 24: C

This is actually a simple puzzle—put here just to confuse you a bit! The words in each row begin with a consonant followed by "r." So in Row 1, the first cluster in each word is "cr"; in Row 2, it is "pr"; in Row 3, it is "gr"; in Row 4, it is "tr"; and in Row 5, it is "fr." Of the options, only C ("frank") is spelled with "fr," as required by Row 5.

Puzzle 25: D

This is probably easier than you may have expected, likely because you have been doing these puzzles since the start of this chapter. The pattern is as follows: the words in the column are spelled with the first five letters of the alphabet in order. So each column starts with a word spelled with the initial letter "a," followed by a word spelled with the initial letter "b," followed by a word spelled with the initial letter "c," followed by a word spelled with the initial letter "d," and finally followed by a word spelled with the initial letter "e." Of course, you could look at this another way and say that the words in the first row all begin with "a," those in the second row with "b," those in the third row with "c," those in the fourth row with "d," and those in the fifth row with "e." Either way, of the options only D ("correct") is spelled with an initial letter "c," as required by Column 5.

Chapter 5

Puzzle 1: Ms. White—gray dress; Ms. Black—white dress; Ms. Gray—black dress

None of the women's names matched the color of the dress each one wore. We are told that Ms. Black sat next to someone with a gray dress. So she could not be the one wearing gray—she sat next to that woman. We know that Ms. Black also did not wear a black dress—as stipulated by the puzzle (remember that names and colors do not match). So by elimination, Ms. Black wore the white dress. This means that Ms. Gray did not wear the white dress (Ms. Black did). She also did not wear the gray dress (since it would match her name). So by elimination, she wore the black dress. The only possibility left for Ms. White, therefore, is the gray dress.

Puzzle 2: Mr. Chan—programmer; Mr. Darrow—analyst; Mr. Farrar—designer

We are told that Farrar makes more money than the programmer (Clue 1). So he is not the programmer. We are told that Darrow gets along with the programmer (Clue 2). So he cannot be the programmer, either. This leaves Chan as the only possibility for programmer. Next we are told that the analyst earns the least (Clue 3). We know that Farrar does not earn the least (Clue 1). So Farrar is definitely not the analyst. This means that he is the designer. This leaves Darrow as the analyst.

Puzzle 3: Spy—father; Geek—mother; Bo—son; Jo—daughter

We are told that Geek is older than the father. Logically, only the mother can be older than the father. So Geek is the mother. Bo is younger than his sister. This means that he is her brother and his parents' son. The rest is straightforward. We have identified the mother as Geek, so the other female, Jo (as we are told), must be the daughter. This leaves Spy as the father.

Puzzle 4: Bertha—guitarist; Paula—drummer; Rhonda—singer; Sheila—pianist

We can eliminate Bertha and Paula as the singer, since the two of them went to see the singer, whomever it is, perform with "the hottest band in town." Paula is also not the guitarist or pianist, with whom she is friends. So by elimination, the only possibility left for Paula is drummer. Bertha is not the pianist, since she plays often with that person, as we are told. We have already deduced that she is not the singer or drummer, so she is the guitarist. Now let's focus on Rhonda. She is neither the drummer nor the guitarist—we just unraveled who they were, Paula and Bertha, respectively. We are told that she performs with the pianist. So we can eliminate that possibility as well. This leaves Rhonda as the singer. Who's left for the pianist? It's Sheila.

Puzzle 5: Kayla—computer scientist; Lauren—chemist; Paul—geophysicist; Patricia—mathematician; Jane—biologist; Maria—anthropologist

According to Clue 1, there are four people who teach at MIT—the first three are Kayla, Lauren, Jane, and the fourth one is the mathematician. Paul and Maria teach at Princeton (Clues 2 and 3) so they are excluded, which only leaves Patricia. So she's the mathematician.

Let's deal with Paul, the only male in the group. He is not the mathematician (Patricia is). He cannot be the computer scientist, the anthropologist, or the chemist, since he sat around the table with them (Clue 5). We can eliminate him as the biologist, who is a female (Clue 4). This leaves geophysicist as the only possibility for Paul.

Now let's focus on Jane. She is not the geophysicist (Paul is) or the mathematician (Patricia is). Around the dinner table Jane is seated with the computer scientist, the anthropologist, and the chemist. So we can safely eliminate her as being any of these. This leaves biologist as the only possibility for Jane.

Consider Kayla next. She is not the geophysicist (Paul is), the mathematician (Patricia is), or the biologist (Jane is). She is not the chemist or the anthropologist, since she attended a session with them (Clue 6). So she is the computer scientist.

Finally, Lauren is not the anthropologist, who is her friend (Clue 7), leaving chemist as the only possibility for her. This means that the only possibility for Maria is anthropologist.

Puzzle 6: Alex and Debbie, Ben and Charlotte, Chuck and Emma, Dick and Ashley, Everett and Fiona, Frank and Barb

Let's start with Ashley. Her partner cannot be Alex, since his name starts with the same letter as her name (Clue 3). She is not married to either Ben or Chuck because she sat next to each one (Clue 4 and Clue 5). Her husband bowls with Everett and Frank, thus eliminating the latter two as her own partner (Clue 6). So the only possibility for Ashley is Dick.

Let's now focus on Alex. He cannot be married to Ashley, since their names start with the same letter (Clue 3). He is not married to either Barb or Charlotte because he sat next to each one (Clue 4 and Clue 7). His wife plays tennis with Emma and Fiona, which eliminates the latter two as his wife (Clue 8). This leaves Debbie as Alex's wife.

Now let's concentrate on Chuck. His wife is not Charlotte, since their names start with the same letter (Clue 3). He is not married to Debbie (Alex is) or Ashley (Dick is). Since his wife plays golf with Barb and Fiona, neither one can be his wife (Clue 9). So he is married to Emma.

Next let's deal with Fiona. She is not married to Frank because his name starts with the same letter as her name (Clue 3). She is not married to Alex (Debbie is), Chuck (Emma is), or Dick (Ashley is). She is also not married to Ben, as Clue 10 informs us. So Fiona is married to Everett.

Now let's consider Ben. He is not married to Barb because his name starts with the same letter as her name (Clue 3). He is also not married to Ashley (Dick is), Debbie (Alex is), Emma (Chuck is), or Fiona (Everett is). So he's married to Charlotte.

This leaves Frank and Barb as the last married couple.

Puzzle 7: Mr. Crimson Sr.—maroon; Mr. Crimson Jr.—scarlet; Mr. Maroon Sr.—scarlet; Mr. Maroon Jr.—crimson; Mr. Scarlet Sr.—crimson; Mr. Scarlet Jr.—maroon

Mr. Maroon Sr. does not wear a maroon tie, as stipulated by the fact that no one wears the tie color that matches the person's name (Clue 1). He also does not wear a crimson tie (Clue 4). So we deduce that he wears a scarlet tie. Now let's focus on his son, Mr. Maroon Jr. He does not wear his father's tie color, which, as we just found out is scarlet (Clue 3); nor does he wear a maroon tie, because this matches his name (Clue 2). So the son wears a crimson tie.

The remainder of the solution is now easy. Mr. Crimson Sr. does not wear a crimson tie (Clue 1), nor does he wear the scarlet tie (Mr. Maroon Sr. does). What's left for him? It's the maroon tie. His son, Mr. Crimson Jr., does not wear his father's tie color (maroon), nor the color that matches his name (crimson). So he wears the scarlet tie. What tie colors are left for the Scarlet Sr. and Jr.? It's the crimson tie for Sr. and maroon for Jr.

Puzzle 8: Tina Gray—5; Len Blue—4; Laura Brown—6; Rita White—3; Glen Green—7

Let's start with Tina. First, she is not the Blue or Green child (Clue 1). She is also not the Brown child, who is older than she is (Clue 4). Finally, she is not the White child (Clue 5). So Tina is the Gray child. We are told that she is neither the youngest nor the oldest (Clue 2). So we can eliminate the ages of three and seven for her. Therefore, she is four, five, or six. We are then told that she is older than Len but younger than some other child (Clue 3). From this we deduce that she is five—older than Len (four), but younger than someone else (six). In sum, Tina Gray is the five-year-old.

Let's focus on Len next. We already have deduced that he is four from the previous deduction of Tina. Clue 5 identifies three of the children—Tina, the White child, and the four-year-old. We know that the four-year-old is Len in this trio, so we deduce that he is not the White child. He is not the Gray child (Tina is). He is also not the Green child (Clue 6). Clue 4 says that the Brown child is older than Tina, and Clue 3 that Tina is older than Len. We can thus deduce that Len is not the Brown child (which would make him older than Tina, contradicting what we are told). So he is the Blue child. To summarize, Len Blue is the four-year-old.

Let's focus on Laura. We are told that she is neither the White nor the Green child (Clue 7). She also is not the Gray child (Tina is), nor the Blue child (Len is). So she's the Brown child. She's not three (the youngest) or seven (the oldest), as Clue 8 tells us. She is also not four (Len is) or five (Tina is). So she is the six-year-old. In sum, Laura Brown is the six-year-old.

We are told that Rita is not the oldest (Clue 9). So she is not seven. She is not four (Len is), or five (Tina is), or six (Laura is). So she is three. This means she is the youngest. According to Clue 10, Rita, being the youngest, is the White child. In sum, Rita White is the three-year-old.

This leaves Glen Green as the seven-year-old.

Puzzle 9: Becky—white—latte; Chris—green—regular; Dean—red—espresso; Inez—blue—Americano; Mark—black—cappuccino

Chris ordered the regular coffee (Clue 2). So he did not wear the red shirt, since according to Clue 9 the person who did wear red ordered espresso instead. He did not wear the black or blue shirt, either (Clue 3). And he could not have worn the white shirt, since he got into an argument with the person who did (Clue 4). So Chris wore the green shirt and had regular coffee.

Becky did not order cappuccino (Clue 5). She also did not wear black or blue (Clue 1). And, of course, she did not wear green (Chris did). So she wore the white shirt. Becky did not order cappuccino, as just pointed out, nor did she order regular coffee (Chris did). She also did not order espresso, since we are told that Dean did (Clue 6), or Americano, since Inez did (Clue 7). So she ordered the latte.

We can now deduce that Mark ordered the cappuccino, since we know that Becky ordered latte, Chris regular coffee, Dean espresso, and Inez Americano. So Mark wore the black shirt, since as Clue 8 indicates, the person who ordered cappuccino wore black.

Dean, as we found out, ordered the espresso, and that person, according to Clue 9, wore red. Blue is the only possibility left for Inez who, as we know, ordered Americano.

Puzzle 10: Andy Smith—candy;
Barb Mill—popcorn; Fran Cash—peanuts;
Rose Dane—ice cream; Sam Wills—nachos

Let's start with Andy. He is not the ice cream vendor, who is a different person according to Clue 1. He is not the popcorn vendor—Barb is (Clue 2). He also does not sell peanuts or nachos (Clue 3). So he is the candy vendor. From Clue 4, we can now deduce that Andy is surnamed Smith, since it tells us that the candy vendor, who is Andy, bears this surname. To summarize, Andy Smith sells candy.

Let's move on to Barb. We know that she is the popcorn vendor (Clue 2). She is not surnamed Smith (Andy is). She is also not surnamed Cash or Dane (Clue 5). She is also not Wills because we are told that Wills does not sell popcorn (Clue 6), but Barb does. So Barb is surnamed Mill. To summarize, Barb Mill sells popcorn.

Fran is not surnamed Dane or Wills (Clue 7). She is not surnamed Smith (Andy is) or Mill (Barb is). So she is surnamed Cash. And she sells peanuts, as indicated by Clue 8. To summarize, Fran Cash sells peanuts.

Rose is not surnamed Wills (Clue 9). She is also not surnamed Smith (Andy is), Mill (Barb is), or Cash (Fran is). So she is surnamed Dane and thus sells ice cream (Clue 10). To summarize, Rose Dane sells ice cream.

What does this leave for Sam? His surname is Wills and he sells nachos—there are no other choices left.

Puzzle 11: The second individual belonged to the Maus

This is a simple version of the illustrative puzzle. Clearly, the first individual would say "Yes," no matter what clan he belonged to, if asked "Are you a Bau?" If he was truly a Bau (the truth-telling clan), then he would just admit it; if he was a Mau, he would not admit that he was and also say "Yes." The woman clearly lied, claiming that the first individual claimed to be a Mau, which is logically impossible.

Puzzle 12: The women are both Maus;
the man is a Bau

As we have discovered so far, the answer to the question "To which clan do you belong?" or a version such as "Are you a Bau or a Mau?" will always be "I am a Bau," no matter what the truth. A Bau would say that he or she was a Bau. A member of the Mau clan would hide this fact by saying that he or she was also a Bau. So the man spoke the truth—both women would have claimed to be Baus—so he is a Bau. He also pointed out that they lied. And being a truth teller, we have to believe him. This means that the two women were liars and thus belonged to the Mau clan.

Puzzle 13: A—Bau; B—Bau; C—Mau

A Bau would answer the question truthfully, and a Mau mendaciously. A and B say the same thing, "Yes (we belong to the same clan)." So the two answers are either both true or both false. If they are both true, then A and B belong to the Baus. The answer in full is, thus, "Yes, we are both Baus." If they are both false, they belong to the Maus, but "Yes, we are both Maus" would be true, which is not logically possible. Therefore, the two statements must be true and the two of them are Baus. Clearly, the liar is C.

Puzzle 14: A and B—Baus; C and D—Maus

A and B say the same thing—namely, that A is a Bau. As we have found out, any individual will say that he or she is a Bau whether or not this is true. So is A's statement true or false? It must be true because his wife, B, who is a Bau, says so. As a Bau she always tells the truth. So both A and B are Baus.

From this deduction it is easy to see that C and D lied, since both said, in essence, that A is a Mau, and, as we just found out, this is not so.

Puzzle 15: A—Bau; B—Bau; C—Bau; D—Mau

A and B say the same thing. They might be either Baus or Maus, because, as we have continually found out, both a Bau and a Mau would answer "Yes, we are both Baus." In the case of the former it would be the truth; in the case of the latter it would be a lie. So C clearly told the truth, since A and B would have said "We belong to the Baus." He also adds that this is the truth, making A, B, and C himself all Baus. D clearly lied, making her a Mau.

Puzzle 16: A—Bau; B—Mau; C—Bau; D—Mau

A and B say the same thing, which is, as we have been finding out, "I am a Bau," and one told the truth and the other a lie, since the two belong to different clans, as we are told. Consider C's answer to the question, "What did A say?" He pointed out, correctly, that A said "I am a Bau." That makes him a Bau and his wife, D, a Mau, as we can clearly see by her mendacious answer. C also stated that A told the truth. So that makes A the Bau and his wife, B, the Mau.

Puzzle 17: Individual C

A's statement can be either true or false, as we have found out throughout this section. If he is a Bau, he would admit it; if he is a Mau, he would never say so, thus he would also say that he is a Bau. B says the same thing. So the two are either both Baus or Maus. They cannot be both Maus for there was only one among the four. So they are both Baus. We can now see that C lied—A and B are not liars, and therefore he is not a Bau. He is, in fact, the only Mau. D's statement is true, of course.

Puzzle 18: Brother A

Brother A's statement contradicts Sister A's statement, so one of these is true and the other false. From this we can deduce that one of them is the Mau—the only liar in the group. This means that the remaining statements were all true, since there was only one Mau in the group. The statements of Brother B and Sister B simply confirm that they are Baus. Brother C fingers Brother A as the Mau, and we know this is true, as Sister C also confirms. So our Mau is Brother A.

Puzzle 19: A—Mau; B—Mau; C—Bau

B's and C's statements contradict each other, so one is true and the other false. This means that one is a Bau and the other a Mau. This fact makes it obvious that A's statement is false, since he claimed that both B and C were Maus. So his statement is false, making him a Mau. C clearly told the truth, indicating that A lied; while B lied, claiming that A told the truth, contrary to what we have just deduced. So B is a Mau and C a Bau.

Puzzle 20: Individual A—Bau; Individual B—Mau; Individual C—Bau

This is a trick—it is one of the easier puzzles that we occasionally put in the difficult section, just to keep you on your toes. A's answer, "Suna," can only be "Yes," needless to say. So Individual B clearly lied, and he is thus a Mau. Individual C told the truth, identifying himself as a Bau. He also pointed out that A was a Bau. This being true, we now have identified A's clan as well—she is indeed a Bau.

Puzzle 21: Seven

You cannot assume good fortune! Let's go with the worst-case scenario. What's that? It goes like this—you draw out a white ball, then another one after that, and so on. Unlucky, but logically possible. After you have drawn out all five white balls, there are only black balls left in the box. So the next two draws—numbers six and seven—will be sure to get you the two black balls.

Puzzle 22: Six

You have to assume the worst-case scenario. In this case, the scenario unfolds like this—you draw out balls of five different colors first—one white, one black, one red, one green, and one blue—in no particular order. The next, or sixth, ball drawn from the box will match one of these. It might be white, and then you'll have two white balls. It might be red, and then you'll have two red balls. And so on.

Puzzle 23: Twenty-two

As always, you cannot assume good fortune. So let's go with the worst-case scenario. You draw out all the balls except the five red ones first! Unlucky, but necessary to be sure! There are twenty balls in total. That leaves only the five red balls in the box. So the next two draws—numbers twenty-one and twenty-two—will produce the two red balls.

Puzzle 24: Twenty-five

This is really a version of the previous puzzle. The worst-case scenario is, again, drawing out all twenty balls except the blue ones. After doing that you have nothing but blue balls in the box. So you will need five more draws, making it twenty-five in total.

Puzzle 25: Six

Again, you must assume a worst-case scenario. This consists in drawing out all the five socks of one orientation—left or right. After you have drawn out, say, all five left-footed socks, the box contains only right-footed socks. So the next draw, which is the sixth draw, you will get a right-footed sock and thus a pair. The same reasoning applies if you draw out all the right-footed socks first. The sixth draw produces a left-footed sock.

Chapter 6

Puzzle 1: B

This is a reverse of the illustrative puzzle. The number of spots on the top part of each domino decreases by one in sequence: five—four—three—two—one (missing). And the same pattern applies to the bottom spots: six—five—four—three—two (missing). The missing tile has one spot on top and two on the bottom.

Puzzle 2: C

In each row, add up the spots on the top parts of the first three dominoes to produce the number of spots on the top part of the last domino in the row. Similarly, add up the spots on the bottom parts of the first three dominoes to produce the number of spots on the bottom part of the last domino in the row.

ROW 1:
Spots on the top parts of the first three tiles:
$2 + 1 + 1 = 4$, which is the number of spots on the fourth tile.
Spots on the bottom parts of the first three tiles:
$3 + 1 + 2 = 6$, which is the number of spots on the fourth tile.
The same rule applies to Row 3.

ROW 3:
Spots on the top parts of the first three tiles:
$1 + 1 + 1 = 3$, which is the number of spots on the fourth tile.
Spots on the bottom parts of the first three tiles:
$3 + 2 + 1 = 6$, which is the number of spots on the fourth tile.
Now let's apply it to Row 2, which has the missing tile.

ROW 2:

Spots on the top parts of the first three tiles:

$1 + 2 + 3 = 6$, which is the number of spots on the fourth tile.

Spots on the bottom parts of the first three tiles:

$1 + 2 + 3 = 6$, which is the number of spots on the fourth tile.

So the fourth tile will have six spots on top and on the bottom.

Puzzle 3: A

There are two parts to the rule.

PART 1:

- Row 1: There is one spot on the top parts of all the tiles in the row.
- Row 2: There are two spots on the top parts of all the tiles in the row.
- Row 3: There are three spots on the top parts of all the tiles in the row.

PART 2:

- Row 1: The spots on the bottom parts of the tiles increase by one, starting with one spot as follows: one—two—three—four.
- Row 2: The spots on the bottom parts of the tiles increase by one, but starting with two spots as follows: two—three—four—five.
- Row 3: The spots on the bottom parts of the tiles increase by one, but starting with three spots as follows: three—four—five—six.

So the missing tile has three spots on top and six on the bottom.

Puzzle 4: A

In each fraction, the number of spots on the top and bottom parts of the numerator domino are doubled, producing the top and bottom parts of the domino in the denominator. For example, in Fraction 1, the numerator tile has one spot on top of two spots. Doubling those gives us two spots over four spots, which becomes the denominator tile.

Fraction 4 has one spot over three spots. Doubling that gives you two spots on top and six on the bottom.

Puzzle 5: D

The sum of the spots in the numerator domino and the denominator domino is the same. For example, in Fraction 1, both the numerator tile (2 spots + 3 spots) and the denominator tile (4 spots + 1 spot) add up to five.

As you can see, the missing tile must have spots that add up to six.

Puzzle 6: D

Here's how each fraction is formed: (1) add the spots in the numerator domino; (2) this sum becomes the number of spots in the top part of the denominator domino; (3) the bottom part in the denominator domino is one more than its top part.

FRACTION 4:

1. The spots in both parts of the numerator tile add up to five
2. This is the number of spots in the top part of the missing denominator tile
3. The bottom part of the denominator tile is one more than this (six spots)

Puzzle 7: B

The bottom number of spots in a tile minus the number of spots in the top always equals one.

- First domino: 4 spots (bottom) – 3 spots (top) = 1
- Second domino: 6 spots (bottom) – 5 spots (top) = 1
- Third domino: 2 spots (bottom) – 1 spot (top) = 1
- Fourth domino: 5 spots (bottom) – 4 spots (top) = 1

Only the domino in option B has this feature.

Puzzle 8: A

The number at the bottom of a column represents the sum of all the spots on the dominoes above it. Take Column 1 as an example.

- First tile: 3 spots + 4 spots = 7 spots
- Second tile: 2 spots + 3 spots = 5 spots
- Third tile: 1 spot + 2 spots = 3 spots
- Fourth tile: 4 spots + 5 spots = 9 spots
  Total: 7 + 5 + 3 + 9 = 24

So if you add the spots in Column 4, you will get:
12 + 6 + 7 + 3 = 28.

Puzzle 9: D

The number at the bottom of a column represents the difference between the number of spots in the top two tiles (first and second) minus the number of spots in the two tiles below (third and fourth). Take Column 1 as an example.

- First tile: 5 spots + 6 spots = 11 spots
- Second tile: 1 spot + 6 spots = 7 spots
  Total A: 11 + 7 = 18

- Third tile: 2 spots + 4 spots = 6 spots
- Fourth tile: 2 spots + 1 spot = 3 spots
  Total B: 6 + 3 = 9
  Difference: Total A − Total B = 18 − 9 = 9

So in Column 4:

- First tile: 6 spots + 6 spots = 12 spots
- Second tile: 4 spots + 5 spots = 9 spots
  Total A: 12 + 9 = 21

- Third tile: 3 spots + 4 spots = 7 spots
- Fourth tile: 3 spots + 5 spots = 8 spots
  Total B: 7 + 8 = 15
  Difference: Total A − Total B = 21 − 15 = 6

Puzzle 10: C

This time the number at the bottom of a column represents the difference between the total number of spots in the top three tiles (first, second, and third) minus the total number of spots in the tile below (fourth). Take Column 1 as an example.

- First tile: 3 spots + 5 spots = 8 spots
- Second tile: 4 spots + 5 spots = 9 spots
- Third tile: 2 spots + 2 spots = 4 spots
  Total A: 8 + 9 + 4 = 21
- Fourth tile: 3 spots + 3 spots = 6 spots
  Total B: 6
  Difference: Total A − Total B = 21 − 6 = 15

If you apply the rule to Column 4, the correct answer is $(6 + 3 + 11) − 6 = 14$.

Puzzle 11: Tile 5

The number of spots in the bottom part of each tile is one more than the number of spots in the top part. The exception is Tile 5.

Puzzle 12: Tile 6

Here's the rule: the number of top and bottom spots in each successive tile increases by one. If you look at only the top spots in each tile, you will see this sequence:

- Tile 1: one spot
- Tile 2: two spots
- Tile 3: three spots
- Tile 4: four spots
- Tile 5: five spots

The same rule applies to the bottom spots. Note that these start at two spots.

- Tile 1: two spots
- Tile 2: three spots
- Tile 3: four spots
- Tile 4: five spots
- Tile 5: six spots

Clearly, Tile 6 does not belong.

Puzzle 13: Column 4

The total number of spots in the two tiles of a column is the same. The exception, as you can see, is Column 4:

COLUMN 1:
Tile 1: $1 + 4 = 5$
Tile 2: $2 + 3 = 5$

COLUMN 2:
Tile 1: $2 + 4 = 6$
Tile 2: $1 + 5 = 6$

COLUMN 3:
Tile 1: $3 + 5 = 8$
Tile 2: $4 + 4 = 8$

COLUMN 4:
Tile 1: $1 + 6 = 7$
Tile 2: $4 + 5 = 9$

Puzzle 14: Tile 4

The spots on each tile, when added together, produce an even number. For example, in Tile 1, the total number of spots is ten $(4 + 6 = 10)$, an even number. The exception is Tile 4, in which the number of spots adds up to an odd number, five $(2 + 3 = 5)$.

Puzzle 15: Tile 5

Puzzle 14 involved even numbers; this one involves odd numbers instead. The spots on each tile when added together produce an odd number. The exception is Tile 5, in which the number of spots adds up to an even number.

Puzzle 16: Column 4

Each fraction at the bottom of a column is constructed as follows: (1) the numerator consists of the sum of all the spots in the top parts of each tile in a column; (2) the denominator consists of the sum of all the spots in the bottom parts of each tile in a column. Let's do Column 1 for the sake of illustration. Tile 1 refers to the top tile, Tile 2 to the one below it, and so on.

- Top part of Tile 1: two spots
- Top part of Tile 2: three spots
- Top part of Tile 3: one spot
- Top part of Tile 4: one spot
  Total: $2 + 3 + 1 + 1 = 7$

This number is the numerator of the fraction given at the bottom.

- Bottom part of Tile 1: four spots
- Bottom part of Tile 2: four spots
- Bottom part of Tile 3: two spots
- Bottom part of Tile 4: three spots
  Total: $4 + 4 + 2 + 3 = 13$

This number is the denominator of the fraction given at the bottom. The fraction is, as you can see, 7/13.

The column that breaks this pattern is the fourth one, as you can check for yourself. The fraction at the bottom should be 10/20, not 11/20.

Puzzle 17: Column 3

This is a tricky one. Each number at the bottom of the column is produced as follows: (1) subtract the top spot(s) from the bottom spot(s) in each tile in the column; (2) add all the results together; (3) this produces the number at the bottom of the column. Let's do Column 1 for the sake of illustration. Tile 1 refers to the top tile, Tile 2 to the one below it, and so on.

TILE 1:
Top part: two spots
Bottom part: six spots
Bottom – Top: $6 - 2 = 4$

TILE 3:
Top part: two spots
Bottom part: four spots
Bottom – Top: $4 - 2 = 2$

TILE 2:
Top part: three spots
Bottom part: five spots
Bottom – Top: $5 - 3 = 2$

TILE 4:
Top part: one spot
Bottom part: four spots
Bottom – Top: $4 - 1 = 3$

Total of all the differences: $4 + 2 + 2 + 3 = 11$

This number is the one given at the bottom. The column that breaks this pattern is the third one. For Column 3, totaling the differences gives you: $3 + 1 + 1 + 2 = 7$, not 5.

Puzzle 18: Row 5

The rule is a simple one. The total number of spots on each successive tile in a row increases by one until the end of the row. For the sake of completeness, let's go through this puzzle in its entirety.

ROW 1

- Tile 1: Total number of spots: $2 + 2 = 4$ spots (starting number)
- Tile 2: Total number of spots: $2 + 3 = 5$ spots (one more than Tile 1)
- Tile 3: Total number of spots: $2 + 4 = 6$ spots (one more than Tile 2)
- Tile 4: Total number of spots: $2 + 5 = 7$ spots (one more than Tile 3)
- Tile 5: Total number of spots: $3 + 5 = 8$ spots (one more than Tile 4)

ROW 2

- Tile 1: Total number of spots: $3 + 3 = 6$ spots (starting number)
- Tile 2: Total number of spots: $2 + 5 = 7$ spots (one more than Tile 1)
- Tile 3: Total number of spots: $3 + 5 = 8$ spots (one more than Tile 2)
- Tile 4: Total number of spots: $4 + 5 = 9$ spots (one more than Tile 3)
- Tile 5: Total number of spots: $4 + 6 = 10$ spots (one more than Tile 4)

ROW 3

- Tile 1: Total number of spots: $1 + 1 = 2$ spots (starting number)
- Tile 2: Total number of spots: $1 + 2 = 3$ spots (one more than Tile 1)
- Tile 3: Total number of spots: $2 + 2 = 4$ spots (one more than Tile 2)
- Tile 4: Total number of spots: $1 + 4 = 5$ spots (one more than Tile 3)
- Tile 5: Total number of spots: $1 + 5 = 6$ spots (one more than Tile 4)

ROW 4

- Tile 1: Total number of spots: 3 + 5 = 8 spots (starting number)
- Tile 2: Total number of spots: 4 + 5 = 9 spots (one more than Tile 1)
- Tile 3: Total number of spots: 5 + 5 = 10 spots (one more than Tile 2)
- Tile 4: Total number of spots: 5 + 6 = 11 spots (one more than Tile 3)
- Tile 5: Total number of spots: 6 + 6 = 12 spots (one more than Tile 4)

The last domino in Row 5 does not fit this pattern, since Tile 5 should have 11 spots, not 9.

ROW 5

- Tile 1: Total number of spots: 2 + 5 = 7 spots (starting number)
- Tile 2: Total number of spots: 3 + 5 = 8 spots (one more than Tile 1)
- Tile 3: Total number of spots: 4 + 5 = 9 spots (one more than Tile 2)
- Tile 4: Total number of spots: 4 + 6 = 10 spots (one more than Tile 3)
- Tile 5: Total number of spots: 3 + 6 = 9 spots (not one more than Tile 4)

Puzzle 19: Row 2

This is the reverse of the previous puzzle. The total number of spots on each successive tile in a row decreases by one until the end of the row. No need to go through the solution in its entirety. Just look at Row 1 and you will see that the spots on successive tiles diminish by one to the end of the row:

- Tile 1: Total number of spots: 5 + 6 = 11 spots
  (starting number)
- Tile 2: Total number of spots: 4 + 6 = 10 spots
  (one less than Tile 1)
- Tile 3: Total number of spots: 4 + 5 = 9 spots
  (one less than Tile 2)
- Tile 4: Total number of spots: 4 + 4 = 8 spots
  (one less than Tile 3)
- Tile 5: Total number of spots: 2 + 5 = 7 spots
  (one less than Tile 4)

The only row that does not fit this pattern is, as you can verify by yourself, Row 2. In that row, Tile 5 should have six spots on it rather than seven, since the decreasing sequence should be: ten spots—nine spots—eight spots—seven spots—six spots (not seven).

Puzzle 20: Row 3

This is a really tricky puzzle. The rule is as follows:

1. Add the spots on the first two tiles (Tile 1 + Tile 2)
2. Add the spots on the next two tiles (Tile 3 + Tile 4)
3. Now take the difference of the two: (Step 1) minus (Step 2)
4. That produces the final tile

Let's do Row 1 for the sake of illustration.

Tile 1 (5 spots in total) + Tile 2 (6 spots in total) = 11 spots
Tile 3 (4 spots in total) + Tile 4 (5 spots in total) = 9 spots
Difference: 11 − 9 = 2, and this is the number of spots on the fifth tile, as you can see.

The row that is not constructed according to this rule is Row 3. Here's what the row should look like:

Tile 1 (6 spots in total) + Tile 2 (8 spots in total) = 14 spots
Tile 3 (3 spots in total) + Tile 4 (7 spots in total) = 10 spots
Difference: 14 − 10 = 4, and this is the number of spots that should be on the fifth tile, which has five instead.

Puzzle 21: Column 4

The card's value is twice the total number of spots of the domino above it in a column. In Column 1, the domino has three spots and the card below is a six. In Column 2, the domino has five spots and the card below is a ten. In Column 3, the domino has two spots and the card below is a four. And in Column 5, the domino has four spots and the card below is an eight. But in column 4, the domino has five spots and the card below should be a ten, but it's a nine instead.

Puzzle 22: D

The sum of the number of spots on the first domino in a column is added to the number value of the card below to produce the number value of the bottom card in the column. In Column 1, the domino has four spots and the card below it is a two; together they add up to six, which is the value of the bottom card. In Column 2, the domino has two spots and the card below it is a six; together they add up to eight, which is the value of the bottom card. In Column 3, the domino has three spots and the card below it is a seven; together they add up to ten, which is the value of the bottom card. In Column 4, the domino has five spots and the card below it is a five; together they add up to ten, which is the value of the bottom card. Now in Column 5, the domino has six spots and the card below it is a three; together they add up to nine, which will be the value of the bottom card.

Puzzle 23: A

Here's how each column is constructed: (a) add the spots on the two dominoes together; (b) add the values of the two cards below; (c) subtract (a) – (b) to produce the number at the bottom. Let's go through Column 1 together. The total number of spots on the two dominoes is $12 + 3 = 15$. The total value of the two cards is $5 + 4 = 9$. Subtracting the two, $15 - 9$, you get 6, which is the number on the bottom. In Column 5, the number on the bottom should be 8, as you can check for yourself.

Puzzle 24: Column 4

Did you miss the trick? In each column, the spots on each of the three dominoes are the same as the value of the card at the bottom. In Column 1, each domino has six spots on it, and the card at the bottom is a six as well. The constant value in Column 2 is seven, in Column 3 it is eight, and in Column 4 it should be nine, as the bottom card indicates. But the third domino from the top has ten spots rather than nine.

Puzzle 25: A

We always like to add a twist in a chapter. The value of the dominoes and the cards in each column is the same. In Column 1 the dominoes have nine spots, and the cards are both nines. In Column 2, the constant value is six, in Column 3 it is ten, in Column 4 it is eight, and in Column 5 it is seven—so the seven of clubs in option A is the missing card.

Chapter 7

Puzzle 1: 46

Add the corner numbers together and then double the result to produce the number in the middle cell. In the fourth grid, adding the corner numbers we get: $9 + 6 + 1 + 7 = 23$. We double this to get 46—the missing middle number.

Puzzle 2: 180

Multiply the corner numbers together to produce the middle one. Multiplying the corner numbers in the last grid, we get: $5 \times 6 \times 3 \times 2 = 180$, which is the number in the center.

Puzzle 3: 8

Add the top two numbers in the grid; then add the bottom two. Subtract the latter from the former. For example, in the first grid:

1. Add the top two numbers: $8 + 6 = 14$
2. Add the bottom two numbers: $4 + 2 = 6$
3. Subtract: $14 - 6 = 8$

Let's apply this rule to the final grid:

1. $15 + 12 = 27$
2. $13 + 6 = 19$
3. $27 - 19 = 8$

Puzzle 4: 4

The sum of all the numbers in each grid is constantly 31, as you can check for yourself. To ensure that the addition of the numbers in the final grid equals 31, the number 4 is required.

Puzzle 5: 768

Each grid contains a sequence of successive doublings, starting from the top left cell and ending at the bottom right one. So in the first grid, the sequence goes like this:

- Cell 1: 1 (starting number)
- Cell 2: 2 (twice the number in Cell 1)
- Cell 3: 4 (twice the number in Cell 2)
- Cell 4: 8 (twice the number in Cell 3)
- Cell 5: 16 (twice the number in Cell 4)

- Cell 6: 32 (twice the number in Cell 5)
- Cell 7: 64 (twice the number in Cell 6)
- Cell 8: 128 (twice the number in Cell 7)
- Cell 9: 256 (twice the number in Cell 8)

So in the final cell of the fourth grid, the number in Cell 9 is twice the number in the previous cell, or $384 \times 2 = 768$.

Puzzle 6: 5

Adding the numbers in each column produces a constant sum—18. Take the first grid as an example.

- Column 1: $4 + 10 + 4 = 18$
- Column 2: $9 + 1 + 8 = 18$
- Column 3: $3 + 7 + 8 = 18$

This pattern applies to all the grids, as you can check by yourself. So in the final one the missing number is 5, as you can see.

- Column 1: $12 + 2 + 4 = 18$
- Column 2: $6 + 7 + 5 = 18$
- Column 3: $9 + 4 + 5 = 18$

Puzzle 7: 3

Did you miss this one? In Puzzle 6 the numbers in the columns were arranged to produce a constant sum; in this one it's the turn of the rows. Adding the numbers in each row produces a constant sum—23, as you can check for yourself. The missing number in the fourth grid that will allow the third row to produce this sum is 3.

- Row 1: $9 + 8 + 6 = 23$
- Row 2: $12 + 8 + 3 = 23$
- Row 3: $5 + 3 + 15 = 23$

Puzzle 8: 9

The final number in a row is produced as follows, using Row 1 as an example.

1. Add the first two numbers: $8 + 5 = 13$
2. Add the next two numbers: $2 + 4 = 6$
3. Subtract: $13 - 6 = 7$, which is the final number in the row.

You can check the other rows by yourself. Row 5 is formed as follows with the same rule:

1. $12 + 3 = 15$
2. $5 + 1 = 6$
3. $15 - 6 = 9$, which is the missing number.

Puzzle 9: 5

The bottom number in a column is produced as follows, using Column 1 as an example.

1. Add the first three numbers: $2 + 4 + 3 = 9$
2. Multiply this by the fourth number in the column: $9 \times 7 = 63$, which is the bottom number.

You can check the other columns by yourself. Column 3 is formed with the same rule:

1. $8 + 2 + 1 = 11$
2. $11 \times 5 = 55$

As you can see, the number 5 is needed to complete the column and the grid.

Puzzle 10: 5

The numbers in each row and column add up to the same constant sum—23. You can check this by yourself by adding the numbers in each row and each column. So the missing number is 5. Look at the rightmost column and bottom row, where the missing number occurs.

RIGHTMOST COLUMN:

$3 + 7 + 4 + 4 + 5$ (missing number) $= 23$

BOTTOM ROW:

$2 + 8 + 4 + 4 + 5$ (missing number) $= 23$

Puzzle 11

A	B	C	D
5	3	1	2

Puzzle 12

A	B	C	D	E
2	1	4	3	5

Puzzle 13

A	B	C	D	E	F
5	1	4	6	9	10

Puzzle 14

A	B	C	D	E	F
2	3	6	5	1	11

Puzzle 15

A	B	C	D	E	F	G
5	10	1	4	3	6	7

Puzzle 16

A	B	C	D	E	F	G	H
1	4	6	7	15	10	5	3

Puzzle 17

A	B	C	D	E
10	15	6	4	5

Puzzle 18

A	B	C	D	E	F
9	2	12	4	5	10

Puzzle 19

A	B	C	D	E	F	G
5	10	1	4	11	9	7

Puzzle 20

A	B	C	D	E	F
9	6	3	7	8	4

Puzzle 21: 162

First subtract 1 from the number on a step. Then double this to produce the next highest step. That's all there is to it!

BOTTOM STEP:

$12 - 1 = 11 \times 2 = 22$, which is the number on the next step up.

NEXT STEP UP:

$22 - 1 = 21 \times 2 = 42$, which is the number on the next step up.

NEXT STEP UP:

$42 - 1 = 41 \times 2 = 82$, which is the number on the next step up.

TOP STEP:

$82 - 1 = 81 \times 2 = 162$

Or you may notice a visual pattern without the subtraction: each step ends in 2 with the number(s) to the left of the ending 2 doubling on each step. So if there were more steps, the pattern would continue 322, 642, 1282, etc.

Puzzle 22: 18

In each column, the bottom number is the sum of the top three.

Column 1: The first three numbers add up as follows: $2 + 5 + 11 = 18$, which is the number that A represents.

Column 2: A (18) is at the top, and when added to the two numbers below it $(18 + 9 + 12)$ we get the bottom number, 39.

Column 3: Here is the arithmetic for this column: $7 + 15 + 18 = 40$.

Column 4: And here is the arithmetic for this column: $16 + 18 + 4 = 38$.

Puzzle 23: 144

This is actually a simple one. All you have to do is multiply the numbers on the vertices to get the central number. So in the last triangle, we multiply the three vertices: $2 \times 8 \times 9 = 144$.

Puzzle 24: 16

This one is a trick puzzle! The numbers in the cells of Grid 2 are twice those of the corresponding cells in Grid 1. That's all there is to it! The number missing from Grid 2 is double the number in the corresponding cell of Grid 1, namely, 8: so $8 \times 2 = 16$.

Puzzle 25: 40

This is actually easy as well, once you get the pattern, of course. The number in each successive cell in a column is double the one above it. So in Column 7:

- First cell: 5
- Second cell: $5 \times 2 = 10$
- Third cell: $10 \times 2 = 20$
- Fourth cell: $20 \times 2 = 40$ (missing number)

Chapter 8

Puzzle 1: Alina

This is a very simple deduction. All the statements were true. So the ones who say they are innocent are indeed innocent. These are Andy, Art, Alexa, and Ariana. Who does this leave? Alina. She also told the truth—Alexa, as she says, is indeed innocent. But this changes nothing. Alina is our culprit.

Puzzle 2: Brent

Here's another simple one. All the statements were false. So the person accused in a statement is, contrarily, innocent. Let's go through who the accused ones are: Ben (accused by Bob), Barb (accused by Brent), Bob (accused by Bertha), and Bertha (accused by Ben). So these four are, contrarily, all innocent. Who does this leave? Brent. So he's our robber. Incidentally, Barb's statement, "I don't know who did it," changes nothing. It is simply false according to what we are told.

Puzzle 3: Chuck

The statements made by Cam and Charlotte indicate the same thing—namely, that Cam is innocent. So they are logically both true or both false. They cannot be both false because there was only one false statement in the set. So they are both true. Similarly, the statements made by Carroll and Claudia indicate the same thing—namely, that Carroll is innocent. Again, they must be both true or both false. They cannot be both false because there was only one false statement in the set. So they are both true. We have now identified the four true statements. This leaves Chuck's statement as the only false one. So, contrary to what he says, Chuck is our culprit, since we are told that the embezzler was also the only liar.

Puzzle 4: Eric

The statements made by Evan, Elana, and Emma indicate the same thing—namely, that Elvira is the killer. So they are logically all true or all false. They cannot be true because there were only two, not three, true statements in the set. So they are all false. This means two things: (a) Elvira is not the killer, contrary to what they say; (b) the statements by Eric and Elvira were the two true ones. So Eric or Elvira is the killer, since we are told that the killer was one of the two who told the truth. We have already deduced that Elvira is not the killer. So it is Eric. By the way, both Eric and Elvira truthfully state that Evan lied—as we know. But this changes nothing. We have our killer.

Puzzle 5: Frank

The statement made by Frank and the one made by Felicia contradict each other—Felicia says she is innocent, while Frank points the finger at her. So one is true and the other false. Similarly, the statement made by Fanny and the one made by Faustus contradict each other—Faustus says he is innocent, while Fanny points the finger at him. So one is true and the other false. In these four statements, considered together, there are, therefore, two true and two false statements—we're not sure which is which, for now. What this means, though, is that the third missing truthful statement belongs to Filomena. She fingers Frank, and, being a truthful statement, we now have our robber. You can now identify the other truth tellers and the liars on your own, if you so wish.

Puzzle 6: Gabby

This is a version of the previous puzzle. The statement made by Grant and the one made by Gail contradict each other—Grant says he is innocent, while Gail points the finger at him. So one is true and the other false. Similarly, the statement made by Glenda and the one made by Gaston contradict each other—Glenda says she is innocent, while Gaston points the finger at her. So one is true and the other false. In these four statements, considered together, there are, therefore, two true and two false statements—as above, we're not sure which is which for now. What this means, though, is that the third missing false statement belongs to Gabby. Despite her declaration of innocence, we now have our killer. You can now identify the other truth tellers and the liars on your own, if you wish.

Puzzle 7: Hank

This is easier than it seems. The statements made by Hank, Helen, and Hubert indicate the same thing—namely, that Hank is innocent. So they are logically all true or all false. They cannot be true because there were only two, not three, true statements in the set. So they are all false. This means we have identified our killer—it's Hank. His claim of innocence is false and he is thus our killer. The remaining two statements by Harry and Hanna are the two true ones. Both truthfully claim innocence.

Puzzle 8: Ivan

Inez and Irene say the same thing—namely, that Inez is innocent. Iris and Ivan contradict this, saying that Inez is guilty. In these four statements, considered together, there are two true and two false statements—we're not sure which is which for now. The third false statement in the set was made by Ida. She says that Ivan is innocent. This is a false statement, so, contrary to what Ida says, Ivan is our culprit.

Puzzle 9: Jack

The statements made by Jack, Jane, and Jill indicate the same thing—namely, that Jane is innocent. They are logically all true or all false. They cannot be false because there were only two false statements in the set. So, they are all true and thus, Jane is innocent. This means that one of the other two is the hacker since, as we are told, the hacker was one of the truth tellers. It also means that the statements by Jim and Jenna are the two false ones. Let's consider each one. Jim says, "Jane did it." As we now know, this is patently false, but it does not help us much. Consider Jenna's statement, "Jack is innocent." As we know, this is also a false statement. So, contrary to what Jenna says, Jack is our hacker. As expected, he was a truth teller.

Puzzle 10: Kayla

The statements made by Kyle and Kayla contradict each other—Kyle says he is innocent, while Kayla points the finger at him. So one is true and the other false. Similarly, the statements made by Karen and Ken contradict each other—Karen says she is innocent, while Ken points the finger at her. So one is true and the other false. In these four statements, considered together, there are, therefore, two true and two false statements—as in previous puzzles, we're not sure which is which for now. What this means, though, is that the third missing false statement belongs to Kristina. She says that Kayla is innocent. But we know this is false. So, contrary to what she says, Kayla is our murderer. You can determine the truthfulness or falsity of the other statements yourself, if you so wish.

Puzzle 11: Louise

All the statements were true. So the people who are indicated as innocent are indeed innocent. Who are they? They are Laura (statements 1 and 10), Lisa (statements 2 and 9), Lenny (statements 3 and 8), and Linda (statements 4 and 7). Who does this leave? Louise. Her two statements (5 and 6) change nothing. She simply says, truthfully, that Laura and Linda told the truth. She is still our killer.

Puzzle 12: Melissa

All the statements were false. So the person accused in a statement is, contrarily, innocent. Let's go through who were accused: Manny (statement 1), Mark (statements 6 and 10), Mina (statement 7), and Melvin (statement 3). So these four are, contrarily, all innocent. Who does this leave? Melissa. That's all there is to it. All the other statements ("I never lie") are false, of course, but irrelevant.

Puzzle 13: Nora

Statements 1 and 9 indicate the same thing—namely, that Nick is innocent. So they are both true or both false. They cannot be both false because there was only one false statement in the set. They must both be true. Similarly, statements 2 and 10 indicate the same thing—namely, that Nando is innocent. Like the previous two, these must be logically true. Similarly again, statements 3 and 7 indicate the same thing— that Nathan is innocent. So these are also true. Statements 4 and 8 indicate the same thing—that Nina is innocent. So these are true as well. This leaves Nora as the liar. Her statement (5) that she didn't do it is false, of course. And her statement (6) that Nick didn't do it is true but changes nothing.

Puzzle 14: Pat

Statements 1, 3, 5, and 10 indicate the same thing—namely, that Pina is innocent. These four statements are either all true or all false. They cannot be false since there were three, not four, false statements in the set. So they are all true. These statements also eliminate Pina as the culprit. This means that Pat's statement (7) is false—Pina is innocent contrary to what Pat says. The fact that Pat lied is confirmed by Paul's statement (2), Parth's statement (9), and Pina's statement (4). We now have identified all seven true statements—1, 2, 3, 4, 5, 9, 10. We also know that statement 7 is false, and we can now conclude that the two remaining statements, 6 and 8, are false. The key one is statement (8), "I didn't do it," made by Pat, which is false. So, contrary to what he says, Pat is our culprit. Statement (6), made by Pete, is also clearly false since, contrary to what he says, Pat is indeed our culprit.

Puzzle 15: Rita

Statements 1 and 3 contradict each other, as you can see for yourself. So one is true and the other false. Similarly, statements 2 and 9 contradict each other. Again, logically, one is true and the other false. Continuing in this way, we can see that statements 4 and 10 also contradict each other. And again, one is true and the other false. Let's stop and add things up. In these six contradictory statements (1, 2, 3, 4, 9, 10), considered together, there are, therefore, three true and three false statements—as in previous puzzles, we're not sure which is which for now. But in the process, we now know that they contain the three false statements, meaning that the remaining statements (5, 6, 7, 8) were true—remember that there were seven in total. So what do they say? Raj's statement (5) exonerates himself, and his statement (6) exonerates Rick. Rick's statement (7) exonerates himself, but his statement (8) points the finger at Rita. Since we deduced that this is a true statement, she's our culprit. You can determine the truthfulness or falsity of the other statements yourself, if you wish.

Puzzle 16: Sandra

Samuel's statement (5) is true—as we are told as well. Since each individual made a true and a false statement, his second statement (6) is his false one. It says that Shane is the robber. So, contrary to what it says, Shane is not the robber and we can eliminate him from the list of suspects. We can also see that Shane's statement (1) is true. Which means his statement (2) is false, eliminating Steve. Steve's statement (7) is true—as we are told there were indeed five false statements in the set. This means his second statement (8) is his false one. It says that Sheila is the robber. So, contrary to what it says, Sheila is not the robber and we can eliminate her from the list of suspects. We can also see that Sheila's statement (3) is true, as is Sandra's statement (9). What have we got so far? Well, we have identified the five true statements—1, 3, 5, 7, and 9. The false ones are 2, 4, 6, 8, and 10. Look at statement 10. Sandra says she didn't do it. But we now know this is false. So, contrary to what she says, she's our culprit. You can determine the truthfulness or falsity of the other statements yourself, if you so wish.

Puzzle 17: Tina

Statements 1, 3, and 10 indicate the same thing—namely, that Tanya is innocent. So, they are all true or all false. They cannot be false because there were only two false ones in the set. They must all be true. Moreover, they exonerate Tanya as the culprit. Statements 5 and 7 finger Tanya. But we know that this is false. So we have just identified the two false statements in the set. This means that the remaining statements are all true. Statement 2, being true, exonerates Tilly. Similarly, statement 4, being true, exonerates Tricia. And statement 6, again being true, exonerates Tom. Who does this leave? Tina. Note that statements 8 and 10 are clearly true (Tilly and Tanya are innocent, as they claim).

Puzzle 18: Valerie

Statements 1 and 9 contradict each other, as you can see for yourself. So one is true and the other false, but we do not know which is which for now. Similarly, statements 3 and 7 contradict each other, as you can see for yourself. So one is true and the other false, but we do not know which is which for now. Statements 4 and 5 contradict each other, as you can see for yourself. So one is true and the other false, but we do not know which is which for now. So far, we have identified three true statements and three false ones, but we do not know which is which in the mix of statements 1, 3, 4, 5, 7, and 9. Statement 2 is true, as we are also told. So is statement 10, also as we are told. Adding these two true statements to the other three in the mix just mentioned, we can conclude that the two remaining statements—6 and 8—are false ones. Valerie utters statement (6), where she claims innocence. But we now know this is false. So she is our culprit, contrary to what she says. Statement 8 is clearly false—Vick is not the killer. But this does not affect our conclusion. You can determine the truthfulness or falsity of the other statements yourself, if you so wish.

Puzzle 19: Wade

Statements 1 and 9 indicate the same thing—namely, that Wally is innocent. So they are both true or both false. They cannot be false because there was only one false statement in the set. So they are true. Moreover, they exonerate Wally as the culprit. Similarly, statements 3 and 8 indicate the same thing—namely, that Wendy is innocent. So, again, they are both true or both false. They cannot be false because there was only one false statement in the set. So they are true. These also exonerate Wendy as the culprit. Statements 5 and 10 indicate the same thing—namely, that Will is innocent. So, once again, they are both true or both false. They cannot be false because there was only one false statement in the set. So they are true. They also exonerate Will as the culprit. We can now see that statement 2 is true—Will is indeed innocent. We can also see that statements 4 and 6 are also true—Winny did indeed tell the truth and is innocent. So this leaves statement 7 as the false one. It is made by Wade who says that he is innocent, but we now know that this is false. He is our culprit.

Puzzle 20: Zoey

Statements 1 and 10 contradict each other, as you can see for yourself. So one is true and the other false, but we do not know which is which for now. Similarly, statements 3 and 8 contradict each other. So, again, one is true and the other false, but we do not know which is which for now. Statements 4 and 5 also contradict each other. So one is true and the other false, but we do not know which is which for now. Statements 6 and 7 also contradict each other. So, again, one is true and the other false, but we do not know which is which for now. In these eight contradictory statements, considered together, there are, therefore, four true and four false statements—as in other puzzles, we're not sure which is which for now. But in the process, we now know that statements 2 and 9 are the remaining two true statements—remember that there were six in total. What do they say? Zack's statement (2), being true, exonerates Zilla. And Zilla's statement (9) fingers Zoey. Being true, we conclude that Zoey is our serial killer. You can determine the truthfulness or falsity of the other statements yourself, if you so wish.

Puzzle 21

Box B does not have a black and a white ball (BW), contrary to what its label indicates. So it's content is either WW or BB. Since the draw produced a white ball, we can safely conclude that it has two white balls (WW). Box C does not have the two black balls, contrary to its label. And it does not have the two white balls—Box B does. So it has the black and white ball (BW). This means that Box A has the two black balls (BB). The correct labeling is as follows.

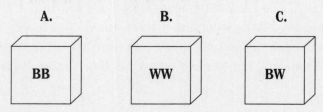

A. BB   B. WW   C. BW

Puzzle 22

We know that Box B does not have $5, contrary to its label. The eight dollars that were drawn from it also allow us to conclude that it does not have the single $1, of course. So by exclusion, it has the $20. This means that Box A has neither the $1 (contrary to its label) or the $20 (Box B does). So it has the $5. This leaves the $1 in Box C. The correct labeling is as follows.

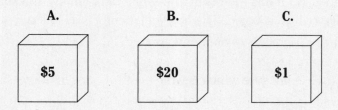

Puzzle 23

We know that Box B does not contain the four white balls, contrary to what its label indicates. So it has either the four black balls or the two black and two white balls. Since a white ball was drawn from it, it obviously cannot have the four black balls. What's left? Two black and two white balls. The rest is easy. Box C is mislabeled BBBB, and we know it does not have this content. It also does not have BBWW— Box B does. So it has the four white balls. This means the four black balls are in Box A. The correct labeling is as follows.

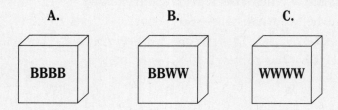

Puzzle 24

We know that Box A does not have BW in it, contrary to its label. So it has either the white ball (W) or the three black and one white ball (BBBW) in it. Since a black ball was drawn from it, it obviously does not have the single white (W). So it has the three black and one white ball in it. Box B does not have the single white ball in it, contrary to its label. And it does not have the three black and one white ball in it—Box A does. So it has the black and white ball. Finally, the single white ball is in Box C. The correct labeling is as follows.

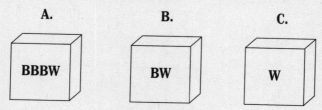

Puzzle 25

We know that Box C does not contain the single black ball (B), contrary to what its label says. So it has either the single white ball (W) or the black and white ball (BW). Since a black ball was drawn from it, we can exclude the single white and conclude that it has the black and white ball in it. Box B is mislabeled as W, and it does not have BW (Box C does). So it has the single black ball in it. This means that the white ball is in Box A. The correct labeling is as follows.

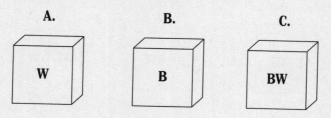